THE MYSTERY AN[...]

IRELAND

GARY CUNNINGHAM & RONAN COGHLAN

Edited by Jonathan Downes
Typeset by Jonathan Downes,
Cover and Layout by OrangeCattt for CFZ Communications
Using Microsoft Word 2000, Microsoft , Publisher 2000, Adobe Photoshop CS.

First published in Great Britain by CFZ Press

**CFZ Press
Myrtle Cottage
Woolsery
Bideford
North Devon
EX39 5QR**

THE CENTRE FOR FORTEAN ZOOLOGY
www.cfz.org.uk

© CFZ MMX

ISBN: 978-1-905723-59-1

Contents

Dedication by Gary Cunningham

For my beautiful wife Deirdre
and our two amazing and very talented girls, Maebh and Darcy.

Dedication by Ronan Coghlan

For all at Teleperformance,
especially Kerry and her pack of chihuahuas

Foreword by Janet Bord

Reading this fascinating collection of sighting reports has catapulted me back nearly 30 years to the time when Colin and I were researching our own book *Alien Animals,* because the sense of strangeness that I felt then was quickly rekindled as I started to read the first-hand accounts of lake monster sightings presented here. Since Ireland has a large number of lakes, in one sense it is not surprising that so many sightings have been recorded. What is surprising is that, despite the existence of all these reports of apparently unidentified water creatures, little serious work has yet been done to identify conclusively what is responsible for them. My feeling from all those years ago that there is truly something strange about the denizens of the Irish lakes was soon confirmed as I browsed these fascinating accounts. After all, many of the witnesses are local people who are familar with the local wildlife and who therefore know when they are seeing something unusual: their reports should be taken seriously. This book not only details a large number of such sightings, but it also provides food for thought from experienced cryptozoologists as to what the creatures might be.

Unidentified lake monsters are by no means all that Ireland has to offer when it comes to mystery animals. There have been sightings of sea monsters all around the long coastline, wildcats have been reported, as well as numerous non-native animals – and Ireland's mythological and paranormal monsters are a very strange bunch indeed. The werewolf and the man-headed horse may seem a long way removed from the reports of lake monsters and other apparently physical animals, but the accounts of mythological and paranormal creatures may help to explain the apparently real ones, and vice versa. Who's to say that some of the lake monsters may not themselves be non-physical? Witnesses cannot get near enough to touch them and are usually reliant on their eyesight alone to tell them what they are seeing. But ghosts are very often solid in appearance, and one rarely feels the need to prod someone to see if they are real – but then something happens that shows they are not, such as them walking through a wall. So as we pointed out all those years ago in *Alien Animals*, some apparently physical monsters may actually be apparitional phenomena, and they may also be capable of shape-shifting.

Some of the weirder creatures reported here are also present in the lore of places outside Ireland, such as mermaids and phantom black dogs, but Ireland apparently has its own indigenous monsters unseen and unheard of elsewhere, such as the Gruagach, the Dobharchú, and dwarf wolves, all of whose nature and existence are very thoroughly explored. The authors have unearthed some amazing tales, and have clearly left no stone unturned in their search for answers.

To those readers who formerly believed that the only strange occupants of Ireland were leprechauns, this book will be a real eye-opener. To those who thought that mystery animals were only found in folklore and mythology, this book will demonstrate conclusively that monsters are alive and well throughout the land, though only some of them may be living in our physical realm. The onward march of the 21st century across the Irish landscape may well have carved a few intrusive motorways into the ancient soil, but it has by no means eradicated all myth and mystery from this magical land.

Acknowledgements

No work such as this can be completed without the help of sundry persons and the authors would like to acknowledge the assistance rendered by the following:

Richard Muirhead, Pap and Catherine Murphy, Tom Joyce, Dave Hogan, Brendan Scannell, Paul Keogh, the Coyne Family, Davy Brown, Martin Runey, Dr Karl Shuker, Dr Darren Naish, Jonathan Downes, Corinna Downes, Dave Braund-Phillips, Dr Kieran Hickey, Steven McCahey, Peter Costello, Tarka King, the Leslie family, Paul and John Mortimer, Joe Kenry, Declan Somers, Adrian Shine, Dick Raynor, Nick Sucik, Patrick Mortimer, Shane Lydon, Yvonne Maguire

Introduction

Ireland: some basic facts

U ntil ten thousand years ago, Ireland was an Arctic waste, populated by mammoth, Arctic fox and the Great Irish elk. This latter animal was not an elk but a giant deer and was not confined to Ireland, though many of its remains have been found there. Splendid skeletons may be found in the Natural History Museum in Dublin and the Museum Building in Trinity College, Dublin.

With the melting of the ice, the first humans arrived. DNA research has shown that most of the present population are descended from these early immigrants. They came from the north of Spain and are likely to be most closely related to the present day Basques.

In the 4th Century BC a megalithic civilization grew up in Ireland and in coastal parts of Europe, of which remains may be viewed in the Boyne Valley. Around BC 2500 a beaker making culture first arrived. These were probably people who spoke a Celtic language, the ancestor of Irish, and who spread their culture over the country through the centuries.

Christianity began to make itself felt in the 5th Century AD. St Patrick [**] was not the only missionary. Although the Irish had

---

** EDITOR'S NOTE: Tony Shiels, one of the most notorious Irish Forteans always maintains that St Patrick was Cornish, whilst the Patron Saint of Cornwall, St Piran was actually Irish. He executed a rather fine painting of the two saints crossing the Irish sea in boats decorated with their eponymous flags.

There is no evidence, as far as we can gather, however, that St Patrick did hail from Cornwall, only that he hailed from "Banna Venta Berniae, a location otherwise unknown" which may well have been in Cornwall, but again may well have not. However, who are we to argue with the one-time 'Wizard of the Western World'?

evolved a primitive alphabet (Ogham), they now adopted the Latin alphabet and it is from here recorded history starts. When druidism gave way, the druids' function was largely taken over by the *filid*, a word roughly translated as 'poets', though they were also historians and gene-alogists. They more or less wrote the prehistory of Ireland, turning the pagan gods into heroes or kings and tying them in with foreign learning.

In the 9th Century the Norse arrived and set up a number of cities. Ireland was now divided into several kingdoms, but a supreme kingship was established by the king of Tara in the 9th Century. However, his hold over the tribal kingdoms was weak.

The English invaded in 1169, making Dublin their headquarters. A number of Norman earl-doms was set up, while Gaelic kingdoms existed alongside them. The Normans soon went native and adopted the Irish language. This situation continued until the early 17th Century.

There was a major rebellion in the reign of the first Elizabeth. The English made a securer conquest of the country and imported settlers into the north-east, but Ireland never became an industrialised land. Its history up to the 20th Century was punctuated by rebellions. The Irish language began to recede in the 19th Century and now, though many of the inhabitants have some knowledge of it, it is a minority language.

In 1922 after the Irish War of Independence, freedom was given to most of the country, but the British retained the north-east calling it, rather inaccurately, "Northern Ireland". The popu-lation had been gravely reduced owing to an horrendous famine in the 19th Century and the country was left in a state of poverty.

A rustic culture prevailed into the 20th Century, but latterly there was an upturn in the econ-omy. Because the country was sparsely populated, people were less likely to notice mystery animals. Moreover, there were great tracts of wild country where such animals might hide, particularly if they were small ones. There may be much for the cryptozoologist to discover in Ireland.

Some relevant facts

- Ireland is divided into four provinces: Leinster, Munster, Connacht and Ulster. Two thirds of Ulster is in the British-controlled territory of Northern Ireland. Five sixths of the country are in the Republic of Ireland, a totally independent state. In older works the province of Connacht is given the anglicised form of *Connaught*.
- The provinces are not administrative units. These are counties in the Republic. The abbreviation for a county is Co, followed by the county name. Thus Co Cavan would be pronounced "County Cavan". County names continue in use in Northern Ireland, but administratively they have been replaced by boroughs.
- In Ireland the term *lough* (from Irish *loch*) can mean either a lake or an inlet of the sea.
- The ISPCA is the Irish Society for the Prevention of Cruelty to Animals. The USPCA

is the Ulster Society for the Prevention of Cruelty to Animals and operates in Northern Ireland.

- Police in the Republic are called *Garda Siochána* (Civic Guard). In the singular one is called *garda*, in the plural *gardai*. In Northern Ireland policing is in the hands of the Police Service of Northern Ireland (PSNI).
- The Irish language is the official language of the Republic. Many can also speak it in Northern Ireland. It may be referred to as Irish or Gaelic, though the latter may lead to confusion with Scottish Gaelic. It should *never* be referred to as Erse.
- For those unacquainted with imperial measure, ' stands for feet and " for inches.
- References to the *Táin* refer to the early epic *Táin Bo Cuailgne.*
- You may come on some references in this work to Charles Fort (1874-1932). He was an American who studied anomalous phenomena. Coincidentally, at Summer Cove (Co Cork) there is a disused military structure which is called... Charles Fort.

Mystery Animals

The world is teeming with mystery animals. Look out into your own back garden (or, as Americans call it more prosaically, your own backyard). It alone will contain not only huge numbers of species of insects, but many of them will be insects unkenned and uncatalogued by science.

Of course, for your average reader, insects are not the most exciting things (though I know one or two people who drool with enthusiasm over them), but if you think of that number multiplied by gardens, yards, grassy patches, greenswards, clumps of vegetation, allotments and countryside worldwide, the number is truly mind boggling. (Was it Shakespeare who said *If you have minds, prepare to boggle now*? Perhaps not).

What most people intrigued by new species find interesting is large animals. Does some unkenned leviathan disport himself in Loch Ness? Do dinosaurs roam through the African forests? Do huge birds with well-nigh impossible wingspans traverse our skies? Are craggy clefts inhabited by hairy figures which are not quite apes and not quite men? What beasts with flashing eyes emerge from caverns in the watches of the night?

Many mysterious animals have been reported from around the world. A great many people dismiss such animals as figments of the imagination, yet in times agone animals believed to be mere legends have been found to be all too factual. Take the okapi, for instance. (If you do take it, I'm not sure where you'll put it, but that's another matter). This creature was dismissed as a native myth until one was actually discovered. If it wrote its autobiography it might have entitled it *I Never Knew I Was a Myth.*

The mountain gorilla was a beast regarded with scorn by science until someone actually shot it. (Tough cheese on the mountain gorilla, I suppose, but at least it proved it existed). When a scientist was shown a dead platypus, he was so sure it was a fake because he believed such animals *could not* exist that he tore it apart trying to find the wires binding it together. The fossil record bore no trace of the existence of the coelacanth for millions of years, yet coelacanths galore were found frisking and frolicking about the Indian Ocean in the 20th Century.

So mystery animals – animals as yet unknown to science – can exist out there. That is why persons these days show an interest in them. Such persons call the science they investigate *cryptozoology.*

This word was invented by Bernard Heuvelmans, a zoologist, who wrote a number of seminal works on the subject. A band of equally interested persons followed in his footsteps. Some people describe cryptozoology as a pseudo-science, but this is only because of limited outlook. Of course there could be undiscovered large beasts. Yet with some people there seems to be a motto, *It is undiscovered, therefore it does not exist.* The platypus man mentioned earlier is a shining example of this. To them I say *Pshaw!* and I say it with emphasis. The only way you can show that something doesn't exist that I am aware of is as follows:-

> If A exists, B cannot exist
> A exists
> Therefore, B cannot exist.

Of course, many mystery animals are the result of misidentifications, misperceptions, whiskey, whisky (the first is Irish, the second Scotch), hallucination and the like, but this doesn't mean none of them exist at all.

The trouble is that each human has a sort of spectrum of what he believes to be possible and whatever lies beyond that he deems impossible. I'll give you a couple of examples:-

Arthur C. Clarke was told by his mother one day that there was a field down the road with sheep in it and that each sheep had four horns.

He scoffed. This, he maintained, was the type of thing you encountered in imaginative fiction. It would be *beyond the bounds of possibility* for such creatures to exist. Then he walked down the road and saw them. This naturally widened his horizons regarding the possible. Yet persons today have much the same mental outlook. (I can tell you, I have seen sheep of that breed and they do look as if they belong on the planet Zonkoid, but they have a firm material existence).

I was teaching a class once and the question came up regarding whether a man could have a phantom pregnancy. I said he could and was believed; but before I said this those students would have dismissed such an idea as an outright impossibility. Horizons were widened once more.

The message I am trying to convey here is do not dismiss anything as impossible without good reason. I have never been much interested in ghosts, but on one occasion I remember such a topic arising. One conversationalist simply said, "Things like that don't exist." Now, if she had thoroughly investigated ghosts and discovered them to be fiction, her opinion would have been worthy of respect. But I strongly suspected that she had never done anything of the kind and that ghosts were simply outside her spectrum of possibility, just as the platypus had lain beyond the scientist's

Some of the animals described in these pages are very unlikely to exist or have existed. Even if they didn't, however, it is not without interest to find what lies behind them, even if it is no more than a journalist's hoax. It tells us something about the psychology of those who report them. It gives us insight into human perception and memory. Remember, sometimes scientists have said things are impossible, only to be proven incorrect. Moreover, by no means all scientists would say all the mystery animals described in these pages are impossible.

But surely, I hear some voice in my mind intoning, Ireland is too small an island to harbour mystery animals. It is not such a great objection in the circumstances that Ireland has a small population and a large amount of countryside. It never experienced the doubtful advantage of the industrial revolution. It is less polluted than any other country in Western Europe. Wild lands and wild waters abound. There is ample territory for unknown species. It is even possible that some wander in from coexisting universes that have portals leading into this one. And before you say such things just cannot exist, think of the scientist's platypus.

Mysterious wakes photographed on the Upper Lake, Killarney by Mrs Corinna Downes in September 2009

1
Ireland's ellisive lake monsters

N.B. – Irish lake monsters are generally called water-horses
or horse-eels in English, the front part said to resemble a
horse and the back an eel, and *each uisce* (water horse) or
peiste (from Latin *bestia,* 'beast') in Irish.

Most people, whether they are interested in cryptozoology or not, will be aware that unidentified creatures have been reported from a multitude of sources around the world. Termed "lake monsters" by the media, the most famous of them is the Loch Ness Monster in Scotland, which is affectionately known as "Nessie". However, I wonder how many people know that Ireland has a rich history of unidentified creatures that reportedly dwell in the myriad of lakes (known as loughs in Ireland) found in the country, both great and small.

Included here is a selection of random modern-day reports from the 1800s. Some earlier reports are included in other chapters of this volume. Also included are those sightings which are significant in some way i.e. details observed, duration of sighting, the very fact that they have never been documented before or if they are very different from even the majority of all other lake monster reports in Ireland.

The sightings and reports that follow are organised by county. As will become clear, some counties possess a far greater number of reports than others., whilst the vast majority don't have any sightings at all. Significantly, the lack of reports from any county in Northern Ireland is striking and I feel there are reasons for this.

- Firstly, with the exception of Co Fermanagh, no other county possesses a great number of loughs within its boundaries. Even Lough Neagh, one of the largest bodies of fresh-water in Europe covering approximately 41,000 hectares only has some vague accounts of giant eels being sighted and unfortunately I haven't been able to ascertain any more results regarding this.

- Secondly, the population of Northern Ireland (approximately 1.77 million) is concentrated in a relatively small area geographically and so limits the areas of wilderness which are prevalent for example, in Connemara and Kerry. It is also more industrialised than many southern areas. Furthermore, if there is an absence of people then there is a greater chance that wildlife in an unspoilt region will be able to thrive without being persecuted by hunting or disturbance.

- Finally, Northern Ireland doesn't possess the same folkloric heritage which does exist in the west. The only exception to this would be Rathlin Island , the territory's only populated offshore island situated three miles off the Antrim coast near Ballycastle. Rathlin has a rich open-minded folklore with stories of *capaill an uisce* ('horses of the water') – there was also a sighting of a sea-monster off the island in 1910 and more significantly an account of a sea monster which climbed cliffs to attack the islanders. I am not certain that there isn't a willingness to accept the possibility of unknown creatures in the North's lakes, but simply that there has never been any known tradition associated with them.

I also feel it necessary to stress at this point that there are counties in the Republic of Ireland which possess a multitude of lakes and yet do not have a great frequency of lake monster sightings. For example, Co Monaghan has approximately 130 lakes, yet with the exception of the incident at Lough Major (more of which later) and an old newspaper account of an unidentified creature in Dromate Lake in the 1940s, I am not aware of any other reports from its waters. This paradoxical situation can be explained by the fact that Monaghan doesn't have all the "correct ingredients" for lake monsters. The most crucial of these factors is proximity to the sea. The county's closest lake to the sea is still fifteen miles from it.

The following examples within the relevant counties are by no means exhaustive – there are many more reports which I have had to exclude as they would have warranted a full book-length treatment on their own. Also, to record every recorded sighting would be not only extremely tedious, but wouldn't, I feel, be any more beneficial in trying to determine what the identities of the creatures might be. Moreover, there are many more sightings of which I am frustratingly unaware.

County Monaghan

I am aware of only two purported sightings in Monaghan. One of these has been written about in the past and is actually one of the more mystifying accounts in the entire country. I am referring to the strange incident at Lough Major in 1960 when three boys – Talbot Duffy, Gareth Reilly and Paul Pentland allegedly saw a monster in the lake as they were returning from a fishing trip. They said their animal was splashing about like a sea-lion and had a hairy head with two protruding horns on top.

The disappearance of captured fish on the lakeside was also blamed on the creature. Previously only one other local person claimed to have seen the creature. Subsequently, visitors arrived in the area in the hope that he would also catch a glimpse of the monster.

The other sighting in the county I am aware ofis the one mentioned earlier which I came across in Chad Arment (ed.) *Cryptozoology-Lesser Known Mysterious Animals.* On page 218 there is a newspaper report dated 29th August, 1944, of a monster in Dromate Lake. The report says the monster's appearance wasn't a news priority due to World War II. During a monster hunt, a local farmer shot at the creature from nearby. The creature made a disturbance and subsequently disappeared beneath the surface. It was described as roughly 7'/2.1m in length with two "arms" which had webbed or closed feet and there was also an 18"/45cm long back which was 6"/15cm thick. The newspaper also comments that local people have refused to fish fro boats or also fish in the lake for obvious reasons.

County Meath
The following report was by Captain Lionel Leslie who, along with Frederick (Ted) Holiday, conducted several expeditions in Ireland in the 1960s, particularly in Connemara in search of the country's elusive lake monsters.

In the 1940s a monster was reported from Whitewood Lake near Nobber on the road to Kingscourt. It was roughly 7'/2.1m long, black with short legs and apparently weighed half a ton. A local man, Denis Naulty, also saw the creature, albeit very briefly. Around 1980 another Meath resident witnessed an object in the same lake that was black, about 8'/2.4m long with three humps.

County Cavan
There have been a couple of sightings in Cavan. In July, 1961, an angler from Cootehill reported a large, dark creature which appeared briefly before submerging in Lough Sheelin. Approximately 20 miles north in Lough Putiagh near Belturbet, Ray Webb (who had coauthored *Fishing for Big Tench* with Barrie Rickards) was fishing from a Shannon Longboat one evening in 1971 when suddenly something caused a great disturbance right beside them. In fact, the commotion was so great that whatever animal was responsible was presumably large and powerful enough to rock the boat from side to side. Consequently the occupants had to hold on for their lives.

County Westmeath/Roscommon
One of the most famous Irish lake monster reports is the one submitted to the Ireland Fisheries Trust by three Dublin priests. On may 18th Fathers Matthew Burke, Richard Quigly and Daniel Murray were fishing on a very calm summer's evening (about 9.30 p.m.) on Lough Ree, a lake which borders the two counties. As they were watching for any rising trout, one of them spotted an object roughly 80 to 100 yards in the distance. The priests were situated near St Mark's Wood on the eastern side of the lake, with the water flat and calm. The object, which was moving slowly, possessed a uniformly thick neck section, which projected at an angle to the water with a length of 1.5-2' and approximately 4" in diameter. Interestingly, the very end of the neck tapered sharply, resembling the head of a snake. Behind the neck some two feet distant was a hump (or possibly a loop) and thus was about 1.5' in height above the

lough's surface. Unfortunately, the object or creature was seen in silhouette which resulted in the priests' being unable to ascertain its colour. It travelled in a north-easterly direction towards the shore and was observed for two or three minutes. It eventually submerged gradually and disappeared. However, after a few minutes it reappeared. The creature continued to move in the same direction at a leisurely pace about one mile per hour, it was estimated) until it reached a point about thirty yards from the shore and then submerged. This episode only seems to have lasted a couple of minutes. The overall length of the two sections was estimated at anbout 6' and intriguingly and intriguingly the priests felt that their creature was propelled by flippers under the surface.

Despite the priests' sighting attaining the most notoriety in the press, it curiously wasn't the only one from Lough Ree.

A retired postman, Paddy Hanly, whose parents actually came from the Black Islands in the middle of the lake, experienced something very strange and inexplicable. Sometime in the 1930s he was fishing with other members of his party at a place called Yew Point at the mouth of Bally Bay when he hooked something. The line, which at the time was the strongest on the market (indeed, it was almost a rope!) was completely run out and the boat was towed across the lake. At some point he had to cut the line and unfortunately (or perhaps fortunately!) did not get to see whatever was at its end.

Paddy Handly's experience, which was indeed very unusual, wasn't unique and other fishermen came forward with their own tales of hooking an unseen, powerful creature in the depths of the lake. F. J Waters was fishing near Beam Island with a strong, heavy line for trout, when he managed to hook something. His unseen catch dived very quickly to the bottom, snapping the line after 70' had run off the reel. With his fishing experience Mr Waters was of the opinion that, whatever the creature was, it certainly wasn't a fish.

Another report mentioned two men who were walking along the shore one summer's evening. They were at St Mark's Bay when they noticed an animal swimming parallel to the shore. Even though it was late, they could see it clearly. The animal had a neck which was raised about a foot above the water. After this came a gap and then a black hump. The men thought that it was a calf so they went out in a boat to rescue it. However, when they reached the spot, the animal had disappeared. Significantly, their description is virtually identical to the creature seen by the three Dublin priests and their subsequent sketch.

Co Donegal
The north-western county of Donegal – formerly known as Tyrconnell, homeland of the O'Donnells – has never featured prominently in any writings on the country's mysterious and elusive lake monsters. This situation I have always found strange. The county has plenty of areas of virtually uninhabited wilderness which are visited but infrequently by fishermen and farmers. In fact, the area known as the Rosses near Kincaslough on the Atlantic coast is strikingly similar to the bogs of Connemara near Clifden and for the same reason: they comprise lowland blanket bog interspersed with countless lakes of various sizes.

Lough Muck in Co Donegal, scene of mysterious creature observed in 1885. Not to be confused with Lough Muck in Connemara, which was the site of a far more recent incident.

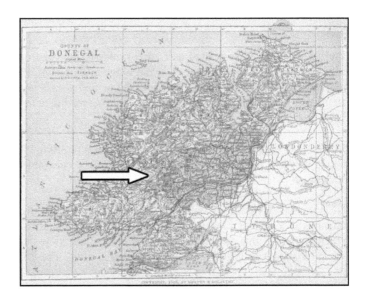

Whenever I first started researching into Irish lake monsters, I was aware of only two references to monster-haunted lakes in Donegal. Both can be found in Janet and Colin Bord's excellent books *Alien Animals* and *Modern Mysteries of the World*. The first can be found on page 201 in Appendix 2 of *Alien Animals* and simply states that Donegal has two lakes reputed to have lake monsters – Lough Keel and Lough Muck. In the Gazeteer of Strange Events at the back of *Modern Mysteries of the World* the listing for Donegal includes Waskel lake and states that a fisherman hooked something large but saw only a yard of black with dirty cream blotches in the late 1940s.

However, as mentioned by Michael Newton in his *Encyclopaedia of Cryptozoology*, the Bords omitted Lough Keel, mentioned in their previous opus. I wonder why? Although this situation is strange, it would be rash to dismiss Lough Keel as a monster-haunted lake merely for this reason. In fact, towards the end of 2009, I was able to examine archive research material which belonged to one of the pioneers of Irish lake monster research – Captain Lionel Leslie.

The Leslie family made not only myself (G.C.) welcome, but also my wife and brother-in-law Seamus when we visited Castle Leslie in Glasslough (Co Monaghan). Lionel's material was unearthed from countless boxes of family possessions by his great-nephew, Tarka King. Subsequently, I received on loan a very large collection of Lionel's personal material pertaining to his passion for lake monsters. Within this assortment of newspaper cuttings, photographs and typed information was, to my amazement, a copy of Lionel's unpublished manuscript dealing with lake monsters of Scotland and Ireland. It must be said that the Leslie family plan to republish Lionel's books (the book on lake monsters wasn't his only one – he was a very talented writer) at some time in the near future.

Within Lionel's unpublished book are hitherto undocumented sightings, some of which I have included in other sections,, and significantly there are reports from Donegal. For example, Lionel reports that a local man who lived beside Lough Waskel had witnessed an animal 14' in length, black in colour, which barely touched the ground when it was seen on land, close to the lake. This was a winter sighting, possibly in the 1960s.

Further sightings were related as Lionel tirelessly knocked on local people's doors inquiring about any unusual creatures seen in the loughs. One man, Patrick Sharkey, remembered the older generation talking about the water-horse and also how a trail of slime appeared after a small lake near Waskel was drained. The trail seemed to emanate from the larger Lough Waskel 400 yards away.

In 1951 Marcus MacCole saw several dark humps protruding from a small lake called Meensbanad which is half a mile in length. The creature emerged from shallow water close to the shore.

Near the small village of Fontown which is twelve miles from the popular tourist resort of Glenties is a narrow road which climbs into the mountains above Lough Fonn. Once you reach the top of this road, a narrow lake comes into view .nestled in a serene valley, which, when I visited it in 1996 seemed to be frozen in time. The lake is Lough Muck where a sighting took place in the late 19th Century. It was told to Dom Cyril Dieckhoff, an enthusiastic and passionate lake monster investigator, who was also a monk at the Benedictine Abbey near Loch Ness. About 1885 a young woman was picking bog bean in the lough near the shore when she heard a splash nearby. She then noticed an animal moving towards her. She made for the shore as quickly as she could. The creature was seen intermittently over the next couple of years. It had two humps which were visible above the surface and, as reported by the young woman, "eyes that were visible about three inches each way".

Lough Muck in Donegal should not be confused with its namesake in Connemara. A monster was seen there about 1885, but has not appeared since 1900. It was described as having humps and large eyes.

The only other lake in Donegal that I am aware of with inexplicable sightings is known as Lough Cro-Leimhne [**] near the town of Carrick in the south-west of the county. I came across the following references in a fascinating book of trivia called *Foster's Irish Oddities: a Miscellany of Strange Facts*. On page 112 it relates how turf-cutters in 1950 sighted in the lake an eel that was 15' long and 8' in circumference, sporting a notably large head. It rose in the centre of the lake three times, as three of the men attested. A similar monster had been reported in the lake half a century before. As of the time of writing, I haven't been able to discover the exact location of this lake. However, its current name may be very different from Cro-Leimhne, as this seems to be Old Irish in nature.

County Mayo

County Mayo is certainly large and contains vast tracts of virtually uninhabited wilderness of Atlantic lowland bog and islands of varying sizes off its coast. In this respect it is very similar to Donegal, Kerry and Connemara. Within cryptozoology it is well known for the Sraheens Lough animal on Achill Island and the mysterious creatures witnessed in Lough Mask. However, there are a few reports from some of the county's lesser-known lakes which it must be said are less numerous than those in Donegal and Galway.

My good friend and invaluable correspondent from this part of Ireland is folklorist Pap Murphy. A native of Cartron on the Mullet (an island that was formerly a peninsula) Pap told me an *each uisce* (water horse) was seen around the time of the Great Famine (1845) in a small lake. Another water horse was reported from a lake near Erris in the 1900s until the 1920s. The creature was unusual as it was spotted.

At the very southern tip of the Mullet sometime around 2007 a doctor and son from Rathfarnham in Dublin were fishing from the shore at Blacksod Bay. All thoughts of the impending day's catch were suddenly dispelled when they saw a creature on the sandy bottom of the sea bed. They told Pap they had seen what looked like a giant conger eel, 20' in length.

The next mysterious creature was spotted by Joe Keery. Joe is from Gweesalia on the Mullet

---

[**] Sometimes spelt Lough Cro-Leibhne

and it was while he was driving home from a music gig in Ballina that he observed something incredible. As he approached the bridge in Belmullet which spans the Owenmore River he noticed a "sea-horse" (Joe's term) travelling across the road in front of him. Joe told me that this "juvenile" animal was more than likely travelling from one lake to another.

Lake monster researchers will be familiar with Mayo due to sightings reported from Lough Mask. The most notable happened on 16th June, 1963. Mr A.R. Lawrence from Tullamore (Co Offaly) told Lionel Leslie about his sightings at this large lake. On a calm and clear day, he saw what appeared at first to be the head and tail of a large fish. Mr Lawrence realised he was looking at two distinct humps which moved across the bay. He estimated that there was eight to ten feet between the humps and the humps themselves were apparently five or six feet in length. The creature was travelling in water which was very shallow, perhaps only three or four feet in depth. Eventually the creature disappeared behind an island.

Mr Lawrence stated that during his sighting the creature travelled 250 yards and it was roughly 12"-15" above the surface. Its skin was black with a smooth texture and there was a wash behind the humps as it progressed through the sheltered waters of the bay. Significantly, the witness described the creature as having "the back of a very large eel-like fish".

The only other incident I have been able to recover with regard to Lough Mask is an experience from Mr Vernon Morgan from Sussex. Mr Morgan responded to Lionel Leslie's article on lake monsters in *The Field* and in particular to Mr Lawrence's sighting. Vernon Morgan's encounter occurred in July, 1963 and involved hooking an extremely powerful "something" near Ferry Bridge. The fisherman conjectured from his piscatorial experience that the unseen creature was an enormous pike, perhaps weighing 80 pounds. (This would be a phenomenal record for Ireland, as some commentators consider the heaviest pike still uncaught to be 50 pounds , also in Lough Mask). Consequently, Morgan was of the opinion that he had in fact hooked the same creature that Mr Lawrence had witnessed only the previous month. Inevitably his line broke and once again proof of one of Ireland's unidentified denizens of its loughs proved elusive.

The Morgan account is contained in Lionel Leslie's as yet unpublished manuscript.

County Clare

Lady Augusta Gregory was, as stated elsewhere in this book, a noted Irish folklorist and gleaned much information from the folk on her estate. In her *Visions and Beliefs in the West of Ireland* she tells of a monster in Lough Graney, which is in the Aughty Mountains near the Galway border. The creature was encountered by a man swimming in the lake and it was similar to a giant eel. The swimmer reached the safety of the shore in the nick of time.

Near Lady Gregory's house was a small lake which was also supposed to contain a monster. Her local informant told her that he was coming home from school in Tirneevan with his two brothers. They heard lots of splashing. They then saw the creature raise its head, similar to that of a horse, complete with mane, out of the lake. This lake is known as Dhulough (the black lake).

There was also a belief that an enormous pike could be found in Gurteen Lough in Lower Bunratty. It has apparently been seen crawling onto the shore to devour lambs and even calves.

County Kerry

The scenically rich county of Kerry (also known as 'The Kingdom', due, it is said, to its wealth of natural wonders) possesses many monster reports from its lakes which are often found in its mountainous regions.

The most celebrated of Kerry's monster lakes is Lough Bran, sometimes known as Lough Brin, approximately fifteen miles from the tourist 'Mecca' of Killarney. There was always a local tradition of unknown creatures in this lake - W. Reeves, writing in 1874, said on stormy nights it bellowed like a young bull - with a black creature with four short legs seen lying basking on the banks in 1940. Another important sighting happened on Christmas Eve, 1954, when local farmer Timothy O'Sullivan went to bring in his cattle for milking. As he passed the lake, he saw an object which he initially thought to be some ducks. However, the "ducks" rose higher and he then realised they were two fins. The fins were approximately 2' long and 2' in height, with the distance between them about 12'.The witness was only 60' from the shore. He returned home to get his shotgun, but, when he returned with his wife, the object had vanished.

Another detailed sighting took place at the same lake in July, 1979. The eyewitnesses were two brothers who farmed near the lake. The creature was black, nearly 10' long and swam the full length of the lake before submerging. The men's father had also seen the creature in the 1970s - he said it resembled a cross between a giant seal and a mythical dragon.

The following account is courtesy of my friend Declan Somers. Declan has an enthusiasm for the paranormal and fortunately for myself for the Irish lake monster phenomenon. As he is fluent in Japanese, he has worked with several companies producing different documentaries. It was in the course of filming one such documentary that Declan met Davy Breen and Martin Riney. Davy Breen encountered his monster in a small lake known as Lough Fadda, which shouldn't be confused with the more famous Lough Fadda on Roundstone Bog near Clifden (Co Galway). This lake is situated approximately sixteen miles from Kenmare and lies in the shadow of Knocklomeena Mountain (2012'/6641m). In 1975 Davy and a friend noticed quite a bit of commotion on the lake's surface. They then saw a long, curved neck of some unknown creature which they likened to the shape of a handle and lower part of an umbrella. Davy has since told me that the commotion was water spraying out of the mouth)presumably) and was similar to the spray from a fire hose. He also told me that his father had a sighting in the 1950s at the small lake south-east of Fadda - Lough Beg. His father described the creature he saw as looking like a pig and it was actually travelling overland from the small lake to the larger one.

Martin Riney from Kenmare told Declan that he observed an inexplicable dark hump in the previously mentioned Lough Brin whilst fishing from the shore in July, 2003.

Incredibly, during the production of their documentary, the Japanese-led team were travelling above Lough Brin when they noticed a dark shape moving under the surface. Although I was initially excited about the possibility of tangible photographic evidence (and video at that), after viewing the footage on countless occasions I now believe the team unexpectedly filmed the effect of a fast-moving localised wind creating a windrow.

I am aware of only one other lake in Kerry where there have been sightings. Lackagh Lake is situated three miles north of Killarney. In 1967, Mr W.J. Wood of Bandon (Co Cork) was fishing from a mound on the lakeside when something yellowish-brown, 7' in length, surfaced directly in front of him at a distance of only a few yards. The creature was visible for only a brief period before submerging.

Mr Wood informed Ted Holiday and other members of the Loch Ness Investigation Bureau in Connemara at the time that a local man had also seen a strange creature in the lake. The witness lived in a nearby cottage with his elderly parents. He told Holiday and Holly Arnold that indeed he had seen something strange in the lake. Near a reedy section he had discerned a small head with two stumpy horns atop a snake-like neck. It had scared the wits out of him.

For details of alleged monsters in the Lakes of Killarney, see below: "Strange Things in Kerry Lakes".

County Wicklow

Reported sightings from Wicklow have always seemed strange to me, considering the county's location on the eastern side of the country. Most reports tend to come from the western, Atlantic coast. This fact notwithstanding, Wicklow has quite a few lakes which reputedly contain unidentified lake monsters.

Take, for example, Lough Bray in the Wicklow Mountains. This lake is one of two as there are actually Upper and Lower lakes. Both are deep and tea-stained by peat. However, a very detailed sighting occurred in Lower Lough Bray on June 3rd, 1963. A man known only as `LR` wrote to the Dublin *Evening Press* stating that he and a friend observed something very strange and unexpected in the lake's calm waters. It was evening and, looking down from a height, they suddenly saw a large lump, which they likened to the back of a rhinoceros, emerge. As ripples spread out from either side of this a head, similar to that of a tortoise, though much bigger, broke the surface. It rose about three feet and swam for a short distance. Eventually, more of the creature's body appeared – it was circular, dark grey in colour and roughly 10'-12' in circumference. The creature proceeded to submerge, quietly leaving an agitated disturbance. Afterwards, the two men compared what they had just seen and only differed on the appearance of the head and neck – LR's friend thought it resembled a swan's more than a tortoise's. In total, this sighting lasted no more than three minutes.

There are also stories of water horses in Loughs Cleevaun and Nahanagan which are also located in Wicklow. Unfortunately, the tales have no specific dates attached to them, so their actual provenance is difficult to ascertain.

My artistic reconstruction of the creature seen by an un-named eyewitness in Lackagh Lake, Co Kerry

County Cork

Despite being the largest county in Ireland, Cork doesn't have many sightings from its lakes. There are, however, a couple of notable exceptions.

As previously noted, Mr M.J. Wood saw an unidentified creature in Lackagh Lake in Kerry. However, this wasn't the first time he had seen a lake monster. Between Clonakilty and Dunmanway is situated a relatively large lake, Lough Attariff. It was June, 1966, the weather was sunny accompanied by a slight south-westerly breeze and Mr Wood was fishing for trout. Unexpectedly, a long brown object surfaced about a hundred yards in the distance. The creature's head resembled a calf's and possessed large, glittering eyes positioned just above the water's surface. The creature eventually moved until it was parallel to Mr Wood. He estimated its length from 10'-10.5' with its visible portion about 5-6" above the surface. It submerged after about two minutes.

The following reports have related to a Lough Abisdealy, which in lake monster literature has been placed in Co Galway. Due to Ronan's research, however, we have discovered that this lake is in Co Cork, near Skibbereen. A lake monster was sighted in this lake in 1854, while the Crimean War was in progress. However, in 1914 a much more detailed sighting took place, involving a snake-like creature. One Sunday morning a young lady, accompanied by her groom and kitchen maid, was driving to church when, from the lakeside, they observed a long, snake-like creature propelling itself swiftly across the water. It had a flat head on a long neck, which it held in an upright posture. Two large loops moved (buckled) in and out of the water as it moved. The three witnesses stared at the creature in disbelief. They were unsure as to the length of time they watched it, but the woman's urge not to keep her Sunday school scholars waiting caused her to proceed to the church while the creature was still visible on the lake.

The aforementioned account was recorded by Edith Somerville (who had co-written along with her cousin Violet Martin `The Irish RM' stories) and are retold in her book *The Suite and the Tear*.

Apparently there was also a tradition of a water-horse in the lake and the lake's name in Irish means Lake of the Monster". In addition, some time before 1914, a local man driving home past the lake on his horse and cart saw an enormous eel-like fish crawling from the water.

Galway/Clare/Tipperary

Encompassing parts of all three of these counties, Lough Derg – not to be confused with its namesake in Donegal – is one of the three lakes on Ireland's longest river – the Shannon. Lough Derg is Ireland's third largest lake.

The sightings that follow are once again courtesy of one of the pioneers of Irish lake monster research – Captain Lionel Leslie. It must be pointed out that I have access to Lionel's unpublished manuscript material only due to the kindness of the Leslie family.

An Arklow businessman, Mr Gerard Kavanagh, saw an unknown creature in the distance on this lough, approximately half a mile away, whilst tending his cabin cruiser. He described it as having a blue-black colour, quite long and leaving behind a wash in its wake.

In July, 1961, Lady Talbot of Malahide was being rowed by a Mountshannon boatman, Hugh Howe. The weather was very pleasant for fishing. However, as they approached Bushy Island, they struck something soft. At the time they were in water no more than thirty feet in depth and the force of the impact knocked both parties off their feet. When interviewed later by Leslie, Mr Howe felt they had hit something similar to the body of an animal, which had then reacted. Even after returning to the exact spot soon afterwards, they could see no sign of a fixed object such as a rock or submerged log.

Other important sightings included that of a retired bank manager, Mr James Ross. Mr Ross, who was also an avid naturalist, witnessed two black humps, roughly two feet in height. James Minogue, who lived near Mountshannon actually had two sightings within a year of each other. His first took place in May, 1980, while he was boat fishing with a friend, J. Melody. They saw a black hump much bigger than any appendage a creature in the lake had any business having near Red Island and, even though they tried to row after it, they couldn't keep up. His second sighting happened in April, 1981, at 6 a.m., only a hundred yards from his caravan. He again saw a black hump ¾' above the surface in calm water, this time near Holy Island.

It was in fact due to James Minogue's sightings that Lionel Leslie wrote to Robert Rines [**] of the Academy of Applied Sciences in Boston with the suggestion that a sonar survey should be conducted in Lough Derg. Leslie met with Rines and other members of the Academy, including Peter Byrne (of Bigfoot fame). Two Loch Ness Information Bureau members, Holly Arnold and Ivor Newby, who had tried unsuccessfully with others to capture a horse-eel in 1968/9 also joined the researchers at Mountshannon.

After testing the equipment in the clear waters of the lough, the team set about surveying the topography, animal life and possible presence of a large unknown creature. On their third day, they picked up a contact on the sonar which was unexpectedly large. They were unfortunately unable to determine its length. However, from top to bottom its thickness was not less than five feet. The team also tried to use underwater cameras, including the famous strobe camera, but this proved unsuccessful due to technical faults.

As a result of the team's apparent success, Lionel Leslie was elated that there was at last some concrete, substantial evidence to support the existence of unidentified animals in Ireland's loughs – well, in one of them at least!

Galway (Connemara region)

The majority of lake monster sightings have occurred within this beautiful region due to its

---

[**] Rines died in 2009, and was best known for his research into the Loch Ness Monster, and the disputed "Nessie" photographs of what may be a creature with a long neck, (1975), and two pictures taken in 1972 of something that has been described as having the face of a `gargoyle` and another image which when massively computer enhanced appears to show a flipper.

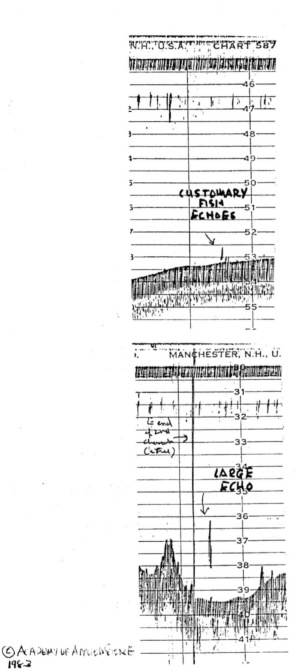

N.H. U.S.A. CHART 587

46
47
48
49
50

CUSTOMARY
FISH
ECHOES

51
52
53
54
55

DEPTH IN METE

1
2

CAMERA AND
STROBE
EQUIPMENT
ECHOES

4

8
9
10

MANCHESTER, N.H., U.

30
31
32

(← end
of 2nd
channel
inchbe)

33
34
35

LARGE
ECHO

36
37
38
39
40
41

DEPTH IN METERS

ERS   RAYTHEON

16
17
18
19
20

LARGE
ECHO

21
22
23
24

FIG. 3

plethora of lakes. There have been roughly 65 sightings to date. Not only has there been a greater frequency of reports from this region, but some of the sightings have happened at extremely close range, resulting in the observation of a greater amount of detail. Some of the following reports have seen little or no coverage whatsoever in any publication and it can be seen that the region's sightings may actually warrant a full book of their own at some future date.

One of the earliest reports I am aware of dates from 1837. Ed O'Riordan from Skeheemarinka (Co Tipperary) was researching his PhD at Cork University when he found the report and appeared only in the Readers' Contributions Section in Nick Sucik's *Mystery Animals of Ireland* website, which is sadly inactive at the time of going to press (2010). The report was languishing in the *Cork Examiner* (15th October, 1847, and rather inaccurately entitled *The Sea Serpent in Ireland.* A correspondent of the *Dublin Evening Mail* describes how he vacationed at a fishing lodge (unspecified) in August. The angler was told by his host that a local man named Conneely had witnessed something extraordinary. Conneely had told that in 1837 he had been fishing in a boat with two companions on a lake near the lodge (about a mile away) when, as they made their way towards the lakeside an enormous body emerged and moved in a parallel course to their own. The men were convinced that it was definitely alive and resembled a huge ball of blubber moving through the water, but they did manage to measure its visible length - 30'. As the men approached the shore, the creature mysteriously disappeared.

The eyewitness saw a similar creature, along with twelve other men. In June 1847, although on this occasion it moved in a semicircle before submerging. It resembled three boats with intervals between, resulting in an incredible estimated length of 90'. At some stage the author interviews one of the eyewitnesses, a young man who provides some additional details. The colour of the creature was black, the circumference of its body was greater than a house and its length was recalled as being between 15' and 90'.

At the end of this incredible report Nick Sucik comments on the eyewitness's unwillingness to regard the creature as part of the indigenous fauna. I would have to agree with Nick on this point as the frequency and terminology used for lake monsters in Connemara (horse-eels) seem to indicate that they are indeed part of the local fauna. This was something different.

One of the most famous sightings to have occurred in Connemara was that of Georgina Carberry, one of Clifden's former librarians. Along with three friends she had been in a boat fishing in Lough Fadda in June, 1954. Lough Fadda (Irish for the Long Lake) is situated in Roundstone Bog south of Clifden. At one point they decided to moor the boat and have something to eat. They were at the southern side of the lake, which contains a couple of islands and it was from behind one of these that a long shape emerged. The fishing party, which included Una Moran, Ann Neel and Arthur Jackson initially thought it was someone swimming, but, as the object drew nearer, they watched an unidentified creature submerge, leaving large rings on the surface. Miss Carberry described it as having two big humps, about 2' in height. The head was about 3' out of the water and the length of the entire body was about 6'-8'. The neck was long and curved, it had a large mouth which she described as shark-shaped with a white interior and a tail that was forked - V-shaped. A couple of interesting points concerning

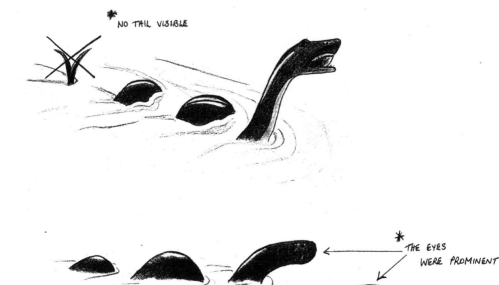

The top picture appeared in various publications during the 1970s and was based on eyewitness accounts by Una Moran, Georgina Carberry, Arthur Jackson and Ann Nee of a creature observed in Lough Fadda, June 1954. The bottom image is eyewitness Una Moran's revised alterations and sketch based on her recollections of the creature.

Lough Fadda, scene of the June 1954 sighting by Georgina Carberry and party is situated on Round-stone bog complex - one of the most important areas of Atlantic lowland blanket bog in Ireland!

her description – first, she was very certain that the creature had movement all over it all the time (she in fact used the terms "wormy" and "creepy"); secondly, her description of the V-shaped tail wasn't corroborated by the only other surviving witness, Una Moran. Miss Moran, when presented with an artistic reconstruction of the creature in *Creatures from Elsewhere* quickly put an X through the forked tail and redrew it with a curved, rounded version. She also noted that the head was rounded and the creature's eyes were prominent.

Just outside Clifden on the Westport Road N59 is a signpost indicating Shanakeever Campsite and this, of course, will be readily familiar to anyone fascinated by lake monsters as the name of the lake in which Tom Joyce saw observed a large blue-grey lump in June 1963 or 1964.. Although Tom's sightings have been documented, he has had several other sightings which have never been published – until now, that is.

A gripping sighting happened in winter some time in the 1970s. Tom was accompanying a friend, Frank Mason, hunting near Shanaheever. (Although *Shanakeever* appears on the Ordinance Survey Map, it is known locally as *Shanaheever* – possibly because of an aspirated letter *c* in the original Irish). One Sunday during a particularly harsh winter – in fact, the margins of the lough were frozen. Frank sighted a dark hump approximately 5' in length through the sight of his rifle. It was about 3 a.m. and it was the sound of the creature as it broke through the ice which alerted both men to its presence. They continued to watch through the rifle sight which enabled them to get a look at in detail. The hump was very dark and moved in a south-west-north-east direction. At one point they watched it move under the ice at the lough's margins. Tom later told me that he thought there was the possibility that the creature swam to the edge of the lough from initially being in deeper water. Tom also informed me that it would

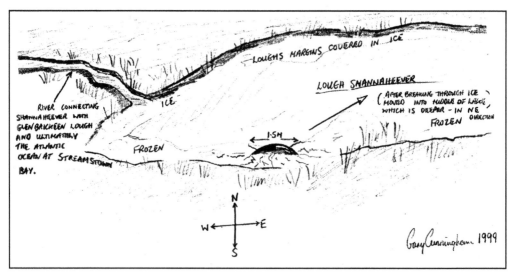

Representation of sighting by Tom Joyce and Frank Mason at Lough Shanaheever in January/February, sometime in the 1970s. The lough's margins were covered in ice!

Gary Cunningham with Tom Joyce outside Tom's former home at Shanaheever, near Clifden, Connemara, Co Galway. The lake in the background is Lough Shanaheever

have been resting/sleeping at the margins and broke through (Tom described it as "pushing through") the ice as it awakened. Eventually the creature continued in a northeasterly direction into deeper water and out of sight. This incredible sighting lasted roughly five minutes.

As significant as the sighting by Tom Joyce and Frank Mason was, it wasn't the only time one of Connemara's horse-eels tried to escape from its icy predicament.

At one time there was a small community living near Shanaheever's famous neighbour, Lough Auna. The cottage (dating from the 1920s and known as Annie's Cottage) which is present in the vast majority of photographs of Lough Auna belonged to Johan Hort and before him it was the family home of the Walshes. On the opposite shore, to the northern side of the lough, the only residence belonged to a family called Mangan. It has since been demolished by successive seasons of strong winds and driving rain. In addition, there are dry stone walls of a small village – the only remains of a small community that existed before the Great Famine of the 19th Century at the eastern shore of the lough.

During one particular winter Tommy Mangan witnessed a strange creature trying to break through the frozen margins of the lough. Tommy Mangan had lost livestock to an unseen predator on many occasions in the past and consequently decided to capture whatever creature was responsible; so, one night, he left a ewe's carcass on the northern edge of the lough as bait and lay in anticipation and some blankets, armed with a shotgun. After a long vigil, Tommy decided to check on the carcass, when suddenly there was a loud splash near to the shore. Subsequently, Tommy shot at this unseen creature, which, not surprisingly, disappeared into the inky gloom, beneath the tea-coloured waters.

One of the greatest disappointments of any cryptozoologist is the missed opportunity to view key eyewitnesses when the right moment arises and ultimately when these key people move away or, indeed, pass away. I discovered this had happened in the case of the Walsh family from Tom Joyce. Paul and his mother had on various occasions seen superficially eel-like creatures in Lough Auna. For example, Paul told Ted Holiday of an amazing sighting that his mother and he had experienced while stacking turf near the lough. Near to the only island, they saw a creature submerge and roll in the water, sizeable enough to create a wave4, which washed up on the shore – at the time the creature was 200 yards out in the lake. Paul described it as having three or four different humps, a possible set of bristles or a mane on its neck and its length was estimated at "between thirty to forty feet long easy". Paul and his mother watched their playful lake monster for 15 minute4s before the mysterious creature disappeared. This event may have taken place in the 1930s.

Paul also related to Holiday that on one occasion he had been fishing in a boat with a friend when a head and neck suddenly came out of the water alongside them. They were so anxious that they immediately rowed towards the shore as they were afraid the creature might rise under their boat and capsize it.

Tom Joyce also told Holiday that two local men whom he knew well were at Lough Auna cutting turf when they noticed something in the water. When one of the men approached closer to investigate, the creature immediately headed for the safety of deeper water. Both men described the creature as resembling a gigantic form of eel – 16'/17' long.

It is very important to mention that I have only become aware of many sightings through my long association, friendship and correspondence with Clifden's resident librarian, Paul Keogh. Paul, as well as being a keen sports fanatic and local historian, fortunately possess an open-minded, enthusiastic approach to the Irish lake monster phenomenon.

The following report is especially true of Paul's willingness to ask members of the library probing questions which would otherwise seem totally irrelevant in an everyday situation.

Sean Walsh, a resident of south Connemara, spoke to Paul about an unidentified creature his father and he saw some time in the 1970s. Both Sean and his father were cutting turf in the mountains at a lake known as Lough Pibrum. It was a beautiful evening with the sun low in the sky and the surface of the lake very calm. At some point, both men saw a dark shape moving at a steady pace across the water. Sean, speaking later to Paul in the library, described the object as definitely animate. Its visible shape and size reminded them of an upturned *pucan* – a local fishing boat 12'-15' in length as a rule. They could see the sun sparkle or reflect water on what they presumed was the creature's back and, most fascinating of all, was a trail of "slime" left immediately behind the creature as it moved in carefree manner across the mountain lake.

Probably the most significant sighting of a lake monster or horse-eel from Connemara was the one spied by the entire Coyne family at an impossibly small peat tarn near the village of Claddaghduff. On February 22nd, 1968, Stephen Coyne, together with his eldest son Paul and the family dog went down to the lough to collect some peat This lake has been erroneously called 'Nahooin' in every single book to include their sighting. In fact, the correct name is Narrawaun. Nahooin is the name of a nearby bog-hole, which helps to feed the lake with water.

As they approached the lough, which nestles at the bottom of Glen Mountain, he saw a dark-coloured animal with a pole-like neck and indistinguishable head swimming about without an apparent care in the world. Stephen initially assumed the animal was his dog, but, when he whistled, the dog came bouncing up to him from behind. He then instructed his son (who was ten at the time) to fetch his mother and the rest of the brothers and sisters. Subsequently, Mr and Mrs Coyne and their children watched their mysterious visitor continue to patrol the tiny lough.

They estimated the animal at about 12' in le4ngth and noted it was black, with a smooth skin texture. Not only did it possess a lengthy neck and a small head (presumably), but, when it submerged, a large hump came into view. There was also a flat tail which appeared close to the head, indicating the creature's great flexibility. Aside from the pale interior of the mouth (also a characteristic of the creature seen by Georgina Carberry) the intriguing presence of two protuberances on top of the head (which Mrs Coyne took for ears), the only other significant aspect was how fast it moved in its temporary home. In fact Stephen told me (when I interviewed him in July, 2000) that in the time it takes to "count your fingers" it had moved from one side of the lough to the other – a distance of roughly 200 yards. Moreover, the sighting is remarkable, not only for the detail observed, but more significantly the length of time involved. Pat Coyne told me they watched it for three hours. Consequently, the Coynes' sighting is regarded as one of the best, if not *the* best, sighting of a lake monster encountered anywhere in the world.

Stephen Junior told me, when I spoke to him in April, 2004, that the creature made a "hiss-hiss" sound at the dog. The dog barked quite a lot at the creature. The children were also concerned for their mother and tried to get her away from the lakeshore in case the monster might "get her".

Another interesting fact, previously unpublished, with regard to the Coyne family is that Lionel Leslie told Stephen Coyne he would buy his cottage for whatever price he asked, so he could prove the existence of lake monsters to the world.

Just over a year later, in September 1969, another lake monster was seen in Lough Narrawaun. This time, however, it was spied resting on the bank beside the lough.

Copies of the sketches of the Lough Narrawaun creature - sketched by one of the principal eyewitnesses, Stephen Coyne Jr.

Gary Cunningham ® with Stephen Coyne outside Stephen's home in the townland of Attygoodane near Claddaghduff, Connemara. The lake in the background is Lough Coorhour. The picture was taken in July 2000.

My artistic reconstruction of the creature witnessed by the Coyne family at Lough Narrawaun in February 1968, Claddaghduff, Connemara, Co Galway

Lough Narrawaun (erroneously called Lough Nahooin) near Claddaghduff, Connemara, Co Galway

A local farmer, Tom Conneely from the townland of Doone (about two miles southeast on the road towards Clifden) was on Glen Mountain 350' above the lough late in the afternoon when he noticed a long creature rolling on the grass before eventually slipping into the lough.

Tom described his creature as very black, bigger than a donkey foal, roughly 2.5' in width, long as an eel and, the most fascinating feature of all – it had four stumpy legs. Tom also stated that the creature when he first saw it, had been lying down and then it "slipped forward" into the water. After the creature entered the lough, it created spray on either side of itself and only took seconds to sink beneath the lake's water.

Strictly speaking, the next sighting didn't happen in a lake, but in Ireland's only true fjord – Killary Harbour [**]. I have decided to include it, because, not only was a fair amount of detail observed and it was seen by two reliable eyewitnesses from different points on the inlet on the

---

[**] Geologically speaking, by the way, a fjord is a long, narrow inlet with steep sides, created in a valley carved by glacial activity, formed when a glacier cuts a U-shaped valley by abrasion of the surrounding bedrock. Many were formed during the last Ice Age.

same day, but more importantly it never receives any mention when Irish lake monsters are discussed, but is somehow always overlooked. What a pity. The full account is published in Ted Holiday's *Great Orm of Loch Ness* (1971) pages 148-9. Through the efforts of Lionel Leslie, Holiday contacted Reverend Edward Alston, who eventually met him at Loch Ness to discuss the sighting. The famous fishing authors Fred Buller and Hugh Falkus said, "Before his death, this lovable cleric probably had a greater knowledge of ancient fishing tackle and early firearms than any contemporary."

In November, 1965, as he was travelling beside the Killary, he stopped his car to look at some seals. However, the seals were watching something themselves – a creature with a thick neck raised some 5' above the water. Apparently, it was staring intently at the seals and remained very still. Alston described the creature as having a head like a large conger eel's, a body the size of a fair-sized car and its appearance seemed smooth. Even though visibility wasn't good due to rain, at the time it was observed that the creature was a sandy colour with the front part distinctively white. After approximately ninety seconds, the unidentified creature sank vertically and disappeared, as did the seals.

The creature was also seen from a different perspective by Claude Hunt, a fisheries inspector

View of Ireland's only true fjord Killary Harbour - on the borders of Connemara, Co Galway and Co Mayo - scene of important sighting in November 1965

from Leenane (the main village at the end of Killary). He described the creature as being between 20 and 25 feet long and at one stage there were two distinct humps awash on the water. As it travelled through the water, Mr Hunt noticed how the creature made a fine spray in front "almost like steam". The animal had moved a distance of 600 yards and at one point it rolled over on its side, exposing three distinct colours as it did. When it was first seen, it was travelling from an island at the head of the bay at which point it moved in a wide circle (which Mr Hunt reasoned was to avoid shallow water) eventually diving out of sight.

Lough Auna has already been mentioned. This glacial lake, three quarters of a mile in length and 40' at its deepest point is also significant from a statistical viewpoint. To my knowledge, there have been ten sightings reported from its waters and considering there are 65 sightings reported from Connemara, then it is obvious that Lough Auna possesses certain factors more than other loughs in the Connemara region. However, the higher percentage may have to do with more people being to hand.

There are two other very notable sightings from Lough Auna which I feel are worth retelling (even though they have been published before).

Tom Joyce told a Dublin student who had been studying the phenomenon in the Clifden lakes – unfortunately his name has drifted into obscurity – about a sighting by a soldier who had been fly-fishing on the eastern end of the lough. The man, who was serving in the Welsh Guards, saw a commotion in the middle of the lake and then noticed a large creature on the surface. It was a warm still day in June, 1977, *not* 1980 as has been misquoted in all previous relevant publications. The man (name unrecorded) noticed that the creature had two horns or protruding eyes. Whenever the man moved on the shore, the creature mirrored his exact movements in the water. Eventually the soldier ran from the lough and, as he turned to look at his eerie creature, he watched it dive under the surface at the deepest part. He was so frightened by his encounter he ran all the way to Tom's house – a distance of about two miles and demanded that he speak to Percy Stanley, who was chairman of the Clifden Anglers' Association. The soldier wanted to make an official complaint – Lough Auna was haunted. What exactly he expected Percy Stanley to do about this I cannot imagine.

Another very significant sighting happened in the same lake in May, 1980 and crucially involved multiple eyewitnesses. It was evening and Johan Kort, who had been a commodore in the Netherlands Air Force was hosting a barbecue at his cottage, which is approximately ten yards from the lough's shore. All had moved indoors, when Mr Kort looked through the kitchen window at something dark moving in a westerly direction across the visible portion of the loch. Along with a guest, Adrian O'Connell, he continued to watch for several minutes as it moved in the direction and cover of some reeds. The visible portion of the creature was estimated at 5' long by 1' high and resembled serrated teeth. Tom Joyce who was also a guest moved quickly to the side of the cottage to get a good look at the strange creature. He managed to glimpse it as it moved into the reed growth. Other members of the party were Adrian O'Connell's wife and William Satler and his wife. They were all local from Clifden. Due to his military training, Johan Kort quickly made a sketch of the creature as, frustratingly, no one had a camera..

APPROX 5FT IN LENGTH

APPROX 1FT
IN HEIGHT

RECONSTRUCTION OF
AIR COMMODORE JOHAN KORT'S SKETCH
OF THE *CREATURE SEEN BY HIMSELF AND OTHERS
AT LOUGH AUNA IN MAY 1980

* — VISIBLE PORTION OF THE CREATURE.

ABOVE: The island in the western end of Lough Auna, Connemara, Co Galway - note the profusion of reed growth which will eventually become squeezing bog. Over perhaps 100 years this part of the lake will vanish as the land (bog) will reclaim it! BELOW: View of the cottage formerly owned by Johan Kort on the shores of Lough Auna - the mountains in the background are part of the Twelve Bens mountain range. The edge of Connemara National Park is within walking distance4.

I spoke with Johan Kort once by telephone during my visit to Clifden in 2000. He was fascinated that other research into unidentified lake monsters was taking place worldwide. I really wished I had met him in person – he sadly passed away the following year.

Whenever I first started researching into the Irish lake monster phenomenon, I was frustrated by the lack of post-1980 sightings and also the obscure reports collected by Lionel Leslie and Ted Holiday. I can now thankfully say that the two situations have since changed. By interviewing eyewitnesses and endeavouring to make the Irish public more aware of unknown creatures in the country's loughs, I have recovered many previously unrecorded sightings. Also, the seemingly "dead-end" posed by the non-publication of reports by Lionel Leslie has been remedied thanks to Tarka King, Jack Leslie and the extended Leslie family with the loan of Lionel's personal lake monster material – especially the manuscript of his unpublished book on the subject.

Examples of unseen reports include the following:-

"One day at the end of a road leading nowhere, I reached a cottage standing beside a small lough and was told the story of how an old woman had lived here all her life without seeing anything [unusual] until one evening she saw an animal that looked like a huge eel, only with short legs, come out of the water and go back again."

"Another time a middle-aged prosperous-looking farmer told me how he had once seen a water-horse, as he called it, breaking through the ice."

I wonder if this refers to Tommy Mangan's experience at Lough Auna.

There are certain times (in fact, quite a lot) when Lionel's humour, intentional or otherwise, shines through. A good example of this is when he set off 7.5 pounds of gelignite at Lough Fadda. When he phoned the County Engineer in Galway to inform him of the intended experiment, the Engineer told him he must be mad. Lionel writes in his book, "To be considered mad in Ireland means something; it puts one in the top grade." He continues, "If I am looked upon as mad, then I may as well live up to my reputation." He finishes by saying, "Anyway, a man who has not done something at least slightly mad in his lifetime has not really lived." Quite so!

Depending on a person's sense of humour, the next reference is quite funny. Leslie talks about the group of people who helped him during his first expedition to Connemara. One of his group was, as he put it, a "poetess of distraction" – Anne Lewis-Smith. He then recounts how they first met on Mull whilst tending to a sick sheep at the side of the road. "She was full of zest and energy, as well as being very hefty – a great addition to our small team." What a wonderful eccentric he must have been!

The next sightings are particularly important as they occurred in a lake that I was only aware of from a single reference in Professor Roy Mackal's *The Monsters of Loch Ness*. In a chapter simply entitles "Ireland 1968" he states that quite a number of Irish lakes have Irish have had observations of unidentified aquatic animals. Amongst others, he lists Glandalough. It must be stressed that I believe Mackal is referring to a lake near the village of Recess, Connemara, known as Glendollagh and not the more famous Glendalough in Co Wicklow. Interestingly, there is an area of virtually uninhabited wilderness south of this lake, which consists of roughly 20 square miles of bogland and forest. Most intriguingly of all, there are approximately a hundred lakes within this area – slightly less than the bleak, windswept desolation of Roundstone Bog. Leslie tells us of a sighting that happened in 1966 in this large lake – it is about two miles in length. On September 17th a London businessman, Mr J.B. Marks, was fishing with his son, aged seventeen. As they had finished fishing and were coming into the shore, they were watching a cormorant (a common enough sight which all fishermen notice). As they approached nearer to it in a boat which had an outboard motor, it flew off and then a round head appeared above the water. This head submerged after fifteen seconds. When they came within fifteen yards of where the head had been, they noticed it had moved a further ten yards from its original position. They then noticed that it looked like the back of some animal breaking the surface.

Mr Marks estimated its visible length at between four and five feet, with a fin=shaped feature accompanying it. He remarked that the creature was much too large to have been an otter.

Apparently there had been other sightings reported from Glendollagh Lough (also known as Garronian Lough), including one by that well-known cleric, Reverend Edward Canon Alston. His encounter happened whenever he was on some high ground above the lough. He observed the dark outlines of a *crocodile* moving just under the surface. He watched this amazing spectacle for about a minute.

The last selection of reports within this section is probably the most important of all, as they are the most recent, occurring in 2005, 2006 and 2007. Strangely, out of the last five reports, three of them happened at Shanaheever and Auna.

On 10th May, 2005, at approximately 7 p.m., Shane Lydon (17) from Clifden went down to the

Shane Lydon's sketches of his unidentified creature seen on the riverbank at Lough Shannaheever, May 9th 2005 - There is the possibility that what Shane saw was a wayward seal

bog at the river which flows from Shanaheever Lough into Glenbrickeen Lough. Whenever he was within 30' of the river, he saw a strange creature pulling itself along the river bank. At first he thought it was a fox chasing his ducks, but on closer observation he saw a totally unfamiliar animal. It was about 3'-5' long, black with a relatively long neck and, most intriguing of all, it possessed two front limbs that looked like flippers. (Shane might not have seen any hind limbs from his perspective). A wandering seal is a possibility. Shane continued to watch the creature for half an hour until it "hopped" into the river and swam into dense reed growth in the lough. The creature described a circular motion as it was concealed, at which point Shane went up to Tom Joyce's house, about 150 yards away. Both Tom and Shane then watched – Tom through binoculars – as the creature made its way further up into the lough and eventually submerged.

Not long after this mysterious creature's appearance at Shanaheever, Tom witnessed something inexplicable at Lough Auna. On 31st May, sometime between 10 and 11 a.m., Tom was driving past the pub on the way to attend to some of his livestock, when his attention was drawn to movement in the waters on the island side. He then noticed a creature roughly 5'-8.5' in length – its visible portion dark in colour and showing three distinctive humps. Tom first described to me, when he saw it, how the creature was "slobbering about" on the water's surface. It eventually moved west along the dense reed cover disturbing some wild ducks and ultimately disappearing under the part of the bog known as Squeezing Bog – where the land begins to encroach upon the lake itself.

I feel that I should mention my own strange experience at Lough Auna. (See facing page) This happened on the 1st August, 2005, when Tom and I were participating in a documentary – *Top Ten Ways to Meet a Monster* – which aired on Discovery Channel in April, 2006. As Tom and I were approaching the island side of the lough in Tom's jeep we noticed something about 8'-10' in diameter, ten yards from the shore on an otherwise mirror-calm surface. Whatever was responsible for this moved towards us as we watched from the shore and, in doing so, created a sizeable bow wave, approximately 6"=10" in height. This wave then moved back – not as a result of rebounding from the shoreline, I might add – in a northeasterly direction and into a patch of thick reed growth. Using binoculars, Tom said at this point he could see bubbles coming to the surface. Eventually, whatever caused the disturbance moved to the far side of the island, presumably unsettling some wild ducks. At this point I grabbed my video camera and started recording. I feel the phenomenon was not created by a large fish. (There are only trout and eels in the lough). I am pleased I witnessed it, although seeing some part of an actual creature, as opposed to the disturbance, would have proved useful for identification. To this day I don't believe the explanation given to me by Professor Kieran McCarthy of University College, Galway. I spoke to him during another documentary, *Ollpheist Chonamara* (the Connemara Monster). He suggested we had seen the effects of a localised whirlwind.

The next sighting to have occurred in Connemara is potentially as significant as the Coynes' encounter. This is due to the amount of detail observed and the amazing fact that the eyewitness saw her creature as she was swimming in the sea, when it appeared close to her.

TOM JOYCE — LOUGH AUNA, CONNEMARA END OF MAY 2005!!

TOM JOYCE'S SIGHTING IN LOUGH AUNA
END OF MAY 2005 APPROXIMATELY 9.30 AM
CONDITIONS ON LAKE SURFACE ——▷
FLAT CALM, NO WAVES ON SURFACE ——▷
WEATHER BEFORE SIGHTING WAS VERY
OPPRESSIVE, THUNDER IMMINENT?

Gary Cunningham's reconstruction of Tom Joyce's 2005 sighting at
the island side on the western shore of Lough Auna

On 23rd August, 2006, Yvonne Maguire, a resident of Clifden, encountered her creature while swimming in the sheltered waters of Manin Bay. The bay is situated four miles south of Clifden on the R341 before the village of Ballyconneelyand is special for the strikingly beautiful white sand comprised of calcareous skeletons of Millipore seaweeds which thrive in the shallow offshore waters.

While she was swimming, she noticed out of the corner of her eye an animal swimming parallel to the shore only 40 yards from her. This made her understandably apprehensive. She therefore quitted the sea and continued to watch the unidentified creature from the safety of the beach.

When I interviewed her in July, 2007, she informed me that her creature was unlike anything she had ever seen. She described it as having three humps, dark grey or green in colour, a rounded head similar to the enlarged head of a snake and being much bigger than an otter. She also felt she didn't see the entire animal as more of it was hidden from view under the surface. Most fascinating of all was the creature's movement in the sea. Yvonne told me that the creature's humps moved up and down – it seemed to have constant movement in its body. At one stage the solid humps formed into hoops as it seemed to glide along in leisurely fashion

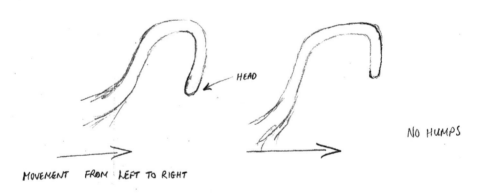

Copy of sketch made by Yvonne Maguire of her unidentified creature seen in the waters of Manin Bay near Ballyconeely, Connemara in August 2006

without creating much disturbance in the water.

Once again, I only learned of this incredible sighting through the good offices of Paul Keogh. Finally, the most recent sighting to date of which I am aware. It happened in a lake which, to my knowledge, didn't have a previous history of lake monsters.

Lough Muck near Letterfrack in Connemara, Co Galway.
This is the lake where John and Patrick Mortimer saw a large dark hump in April 2007.
This is the last recorded sighting (at time of publication in summer 2010) of which
I am aware in Connemara.

On 11th April, 2007, two local men, John Mortimer and his nephew Patrick were driving beside the shores of Lough Muck – a large lake two miles east of Killary Harbour. As they looked out at the apparent blackness, they saw a large dark lump in the water. They estimated it at ten feet in length and protruding 1.5' above the lough's surface. They described it as "pure shiny black in colour" with the slim texture of an eel "like a big conger". It apparently moved around the lough for a moment before it submerged into the peaty depths, leaving nary a trace. This lough should not be confused with Lough Muck in Donegal.

In Lough Corrib, large though it is, I have only vague reports of serpents and eel-like creatures.

Exceptional reports

As with all research into the exceptional and mysterious, there are on occasion some reports which it is difficult to rationalise. The Connemara district has several instances which are very different from the previous selection.

There are two instances when Connemara's horse-eels have been trapped under human constructions.

The first time was at a culvert which allowed the river to pass under a bridge between Loughs Gowlan (sometimes mis-called *Crolan* and *Loughanarrow*) and the much larger Derrylea. These lakes are situated on the main N59 road to Galway, approximately 3.5 miles east of Clifden. According to local testimony a large eel-like creature became trapped in one of the culverts that pass underneath the stone bridge. This took place around 1890, with the creature's appearance described as "loathsome". In fact, so repulsive was the unfortunate creature's appearance that local people let it decompose – their matter of fact phrase was that it "melted away". This was not the only such incident: ten tears later another specimen of a Connemara lake monster became incarcerated under another bridge only five miles distant from the first.

Near Ballynahinch Castle (which is now an hotel) is a narrow road leading to this historic residence. On this narrow road the Ballynahinch River is spanned by a couple of bridges and it is the last bridge before the hotel which is the site of the second incident. This is recounded by Holiday. Holiday, Leslie and other members including Ivor Newby and Holly Arnold met a local man, Martin Walsh, who told them an elderly neighbour could divulge more about the stranding. It transpired that the horse-eel had become stuck under the bridge's span and was 30' long. A blacksmith from the village of Cashel was commissioned to forge a barbed spear to kill the creature. However, an overnight flood saved the creature and prevented it from meeting a gruesome death. The next report is difficult to rationalise. It is unique amongst Irish lake monster reports. Glinsk is a small village located three miles from the River Suck in Co Galway.

In March, 1962, a teacher at the local National School, Alphonsus Mullaney, and his son, also called Alphonsus, had a very frightening encounter from on the shore of Lough Dubh. They were spoon fishing for perch and pike (despite the name of this process, you don't use a spoon) while also using a shorter rod with worms as bait. After a while, Mr Mullaney decided they should call it a day, but would try one more cast before leaving. Both I and my brother-in-law, Seamus Bracken, have often done this before leaving for home). Next there was something pulling on the line which eventually snapped – at this point the young boy screamed. The boy's father then saw the creature. It had short t hick legs, was dark grey and was covered with bristles or short hair. Most incredible of all, though, was its hippo face, with small ears and a white horn on its snout. Overall, the creature was as big as a cow. Mr Mullaney assumed that the creature had taken the fishing bait and had then been aggravated by a dog barking. It then tried to mount the bank and attack the boy.

Mr Mullaney took his son away from the lake and persuaded local men to search the shore.

The Mullaney's creature is very difficult to reconcile with any known animal of the past or present. To my mind, there are two possibilities – either they mistook a wandering walrus with a single tusk, which had somehow become twisted upward, perhaps in combat or they witnessed an aquatic rhinoceros in Ireland.

Paul Keogh - Clifden's resident librarian. Paul is very enthusiastic about the Irish Lake Monster phenomenon, and especially the sightings of unidentified creatures in the lakes of Connemara, and is good friends with both me and my wife.

Brendan Scanell is a resident of Clifden, Connemara. He is very passionate about the unidentified creatures that are seen in Connemara's many loughs

Reconstruction of *Basilosaurus* adapted from *Sea Monsters - Prehistoric Predators of the Deep* (BBC Books)

During the last fourteen years of researching and studying the lake monster phenomenon, I have only ever chanced upon two other creatures bearing a superficial similarity to the very enigmatic creature viewed at Lough Dubh on that special occasion.

The first creature which seems to possess similar physical traits is one reported to Miss Somerville-Large by an elderly acquaintance of hers known as Thady Byrne. He questioned her about "the monster in the woods", referring to a large area of hills and glens in West Cork, which terminated in an inlet of the sea known as Myross Bay. Mr Byrne saw this monster on the way home sitting on a rock watching him. The creature was black, similar in size to a greyhound.It possessed long bristles coming out of either side of its jaws, although it had no hair on its tail. The creature was described as having "a great jowl on it, like a bulldog". It was also quite broad and had a sloping profile towards its hindquarters. Apparently the creature made a barking sound at night, which was likened to the squeal of a seagull. Apparently it was seen quite frequently over the week.

The only other creature resembling Mullaney's is a reference to a beast from the western regions of Scotland. This is the Biasd na Srogaig, found only in the folklore of the Isle of Skye, which is one of the Hebrides. It is a one-horned creature and Forbes uses it to translate *unicorn* into Gaelic. As Scotland, like Ireland, is well within the range of the Atlantic walrus (especially immature males ostracised from the main group) then it is perfectly reasonable to assume walrus and especially individuals with one tusk are responsible for the sightings of the aforementioned mystery creatures. In fact, so unexpected would such an encounter be that the eyewitnesses might describe their beast as similar to an aquatic, bristle-covered, one horned, square-faced rhinoceros – sound familiar?

Strange Things in Kerry Lakes

The county of Kerry in the south-west of Ireland is accounted one of the wildest. It takes its name from a people called the *Ciarraighe* (the black-haired ones) who lived there. The scenery is spectacular. The peninsula of Beare was said to be home to the Cailleach Beara, a hag who seems to be in origin a goddess. The Irish language is still spoken in parts of it and, in days gone by, Latin was quite commonly spoken there. The English of Kerry is often too thick for the Anglo-Saxon ear, especially if it is intermixed with Irish.

It is to the lakes of this county the cryptozoologist must fare. Lough Brin (or Bran) has an interesting set of traditions. It is 210' deep in parts and is about ten miles north-west of Kenmare. Here Bran, one of the hounds of the hero Fionn mac Cumhaill (Finn mac Cool) was said to have been drowned. Bran was, apart from being his hound, his nephew. How this comes about is because Fionn's sister was turned into a bitch and, in that state, gave birth to two hounds, Bran and Sceolan. Forbes gives a couple of descriptions of Bran, both equally bizarre. One says he was dark green with black sides and blood-red ears; another says he had a small head, white breast, dragon's eyes, wolf's claws, lion's vigour and a serpent's venom.

There have been a number of sightings of a lake monster in its depths. These have been dealt with above.

Did Tony Shiels `raise` a monster in Killarney's lakes during mid September 2009?

A strange creature called the carrabuncle is said to dwell in one of the lakes of Kerry, but, as differing names have been given to the lake, it has not been possible to trace which one it is supposed to inhabit. It is first mentioned by C. Smith in 1756, but it appears he thought it to be a stone. Then H. Hart said there was in Lough Veagh a huge animal called the carrabuncle with gold and jewels attached. It was like a snake. It resembled a cask, said another informant, and lived in Lough Geal. The matter is further complicated by the existence of a legendary South American fish called the carbuncle mentioned in Barco Centenaro's *Argentina* (1607). It is supposed to have a mirror in its head, like a glowing coal.

The town of Killarney is situated in the midst of Kerry near a trio of breathtakingly scenic lakes. These are Muckross Lake, the Upper Lake and Lough Leane. There has been a vague suggestion that there might be an unknown creature in Lough Leane, but not enough to pursue the matter at this juncture. In 2003, however, something strange was found in Muckross Lake. The Irish Char Conservation Group were conducting a survey of fish in the lake. They found Arctic char (*Salvelinus alpinus*) but were also astonished to discover on their echosounder an object which they described as being of the size of a two-story house. There is no local tradition of the lake's harbouring a monster. A suggestion has been made that what lurks in the depths is a huge white eel. More sceptical commentators have suggested it is a gigantic shoal of Arctic char pressed close together.

The monster of the Upper Lake was seen, filmed and photographed by Jonathan Downes and his party in September, 2009.

Jonathan Downes is the supremo of the Centre for Fortean Zoology, which he runs in monarchical splendour from Woolsery in Devon. With him were his wife Corinna, rumoured to be the only person able to make him behave, and Max Blake, a budding boffin, currently (2010) reading zoology at the University of Bristol. We learn that Max had been somewhat traumatised by the lack of Cornish pasties in Ireland, but this should not have affected his judgement of the incident soon to occur.

They were holidaying with the controversial "Doc" Shiels, who has led a colourful life. Shiels is a conjurer, but he claims that, as well as mere prestidigitation, he can perform feats of a genuinely preternatural order. Amongst other things, he claims to be able to raise monsters to the surface of lakes.

They were positioned on 17th September above Ladies View gazing down on the Upper Lake. Shiels began to make summoning signs. Downes photographed Shiels' gestures, while Corinna and Blake filmed the lake. Large ripples appeared upon the surface and Downes said he saw something large and white which dived. After this a large wake was discernable heading for the shore. Something broke the surface and dived once more. After this a bird, perhaps a tufted duck, took off. Another object was seen making a wake.

At this stage Downes was giving ecstatic rein to his more than adequate vocabulary of non-parliamentary words. After studying a recording of one of the wakes, he was to say it was perhaps a cormorant being pursued by some underwater creature. His present opinion seems to be that the creature is some sort of eel.

One of the reasons some cryptozoologists may view this episode hesitantly is because Shiels has admitted he is quite capable of hoaxing as well as performing real preternatural deeds. However, two factors must be considered here. There are people who seem to have a genuine power to summon creatures from the water, such as fish and porpoises. Accounts of such incidents have been published. It may be of course, that Shiels knew the cycle of the lake and at what time these creatures might be depended upon to surface for feeding. However, he can hardly have hoaxed the creatures himself, unless he persuaded some doughty Kerrymen to swim beneath the waters impersonating monsters. Unless the onlookers were mistaken or the filming and photography misinterpreted, we have here impressive evidence of unknown lacustrine creatures.

Although these lakes do not have legends of monsters in their depths, a great many Irish lakes do. They are often referred to by the word *peiste/piast*, which is not a native Irish word. The true Irish form appears to be *each uisce* (water horse) and they are sometimes referred to as horse-eels in English. The gigantic eel theory is plausible. Eels usually leave their spawning grounds to mate, heading for the Sargasso Sea in the mid-Atlantic. They then return to their place of birth to die. However, zoologist Richard Freeman has suggested that eunuch eels, unable to spawn, may simply remain in the lakes of their birth, growing ever larger. This is plausible, but some folklore suggests these beasts have legs. We shall have to see.

There is also a tradition of a monster or monsters in Loch Looscanaugh in this county, but we are bereft of significant details.

A creature in Kerry belief is (or was) called the Currane Duv (Irish *crain dubh*, 'black sow'). This was a 15' long sea-monster with a mane. It would be seen offshore from Magharees to Brandon Head and would sometimes swim upriver. Although it was regularly regarded as a sea-creature, it bears no little resemblance to Irish lake monsters.

The county of Kerry boasts a range of mountains called MacGillicuddy's Reeks. The local clan is the MacGillicuddys. One of the mountains is called *Cnoc na Peiste* – the monster's hill. These animals are much ingrained in Irish folklore.

Hoaxes

No discussion of lake monsters would be complete without discussing hoaxes. The most incredible incidence of hoaxing is the alleged eyewitness sighting of the two-horned or tusked creature seen by three youths fishing at Lough major in Co Monaghan.in July, 1960. In his book Leslie states, "As I happened to be there [in Monaghan] at the time I made some enquiries and soon found out that it had been a hoax..." Leslie finishes by saying , "This case is of interest to show how easy it is to start a monster legend, especially when reports of a similar nature are appearing in the news. From other parts of the country.. Each witness should be interrogated separately and in detail before jumping to any conclusion." Very wise words indeed.

What Are Ireland's Elusive Lake Monsters?

In Connemara and Ireland generally the facts are ordinary people are seeing large (sometimes very large) unidentifiable creatures in many different loughs. As for the possible identities proposed, we have the usual suspects within the study of lake monsters – giant freshwater eels. An undiscovered long-necked seal, plesiosaurs and a living form of primitive whale (or archaeocete). To this may be added the exciting possibility that a new form of freshwater cetacean might be responsible, as suggested by both Dr Karl Shuker and Dr Darren Naish. There is also, of course, the misperception of known animals or inanimate objects, such as logs or rocks.

Radford and Nickell in *Lake Monster Mysteries* have a valid point in regard to eyewitness perception of an inanimate object as a living creature depending on certain circumstances. It is also very difficult to estimate the size of an object over water, especially if there are no points of reference. However, after interviewing eyewitnesses in Connemara, I do believe they have not been deceived in this way or even by unknown behaviour rarely seen, such as a family of otters swimming in a line. The familiarity with local wildlife, no matter how shy and elusive, and the relatively short distances between observer and subject would argue against eyewitness misidentification.

Most cryptozoologists would consider it highly improbable that a plesiosaur could have survived the extinction trap and be responsible for sightings worldwide.

However, a novel form of long-necked seal does seem more plausible due to its mammalian adaptability and the possibility that it could conceivably give birth in one of Connemara's many sheltered bays. However, the lengthy tail some witnesses have reported would rule out a seal.

The theory that giant freshwater eels might be responsible for some of the sightings is more conservative and plausible. However, when viewed in the context of the more detailed reports it fails due to certain physical characteristics.

Both Yvonne Maguire and the Coynes saw their creatures in close proximity and in Yvonne's case she watched the animal for approximately five minutes. When interviewed they both were adamant that their animals possessed lengthy necks and were distinct enough from otters, seals or eels, for that matter. There remains the possibility that *some* of the sightings are of giant eels.

These would include the Mortimers' sighting in Lough Muck and Martin Riney's silent visitor in Lough Ree.

Even Tom Joyce's unidentified creature in Lough Auna exhibited the size and shape of a large eel swimming on the lough's surface.as if it had been forced to rise from the bottom of the lough as a result of oxygen depletion which might occur in very hot, settled conditions, as was the case when Tom saw his creature in 2005.

The origin of the term *horse-eel* used to describe Connemara's bog loughs is intriguing and provocative. The term *horse* has been used in Ireland in the context of angling for a long time. Dave Hogan, a wildlife ranger in Connemara's National Park at Letterfrack informed me that a very large mackerel was referred to as a horse-mackerel, so that perhaps horse-eels were nothing more than oversixed specimens of freshwater eels. This still raises the possibility that some eels may be attaining sizes greater than those currently logged by science. (The largest freshwater eels known are the long-finned eels of New Zealand and Tasmania which can attain a length of 2m/6.5' or more).

Couple this with reports from the 1960s and 1970s of loughs where eel-like features were described e.g. Tom Conneely's sighting in 1963 in Lough Gowlaun (miscalled Lough Crolan) and it transpires that maybe a type of giant eel may yet be responsible for some sightings.

A favourite candidate proposed by cryptozoologists for the elusive inhabitants of Ireland's loughs is a form of archaeocete (primitive whale) that has somehow survived the extinction trap. The animals, especially in Connemara, bear an uncanny resemblance to the possible appearance in life of certain fossil forms of archaeocete. An important feature would be the reports of creatures seen on land, where they have been observed with four limbs. This morphological characteristic (quadrapedalism) was only recognised in the fossil forms in 1989 and would therefore have been unknown by the eyewitnesses in order to "pad out" their own sighting of an otherwise mundane creature – such as an unusually large eel.

Maybe in the future a more suitable candidate for Ireland's lake creatures will be discovered.

As mentioned by Dr Karl Shuker in *In Search of Prehistoric Monsters*(1995) a living form of archaeocete would be morphologically different from its fossil ancestors. This notion is based on the assumption that since all currently known forms of archaeocete are absent from the fossil record for 25-30 million years, any modern day descendant would have had the luxury within that the time to evolve. Evolution would then provide the living creature with a longer neck than any fossil forms currently recognised by science. He thinks a living archaeocete by no means implausible and that the only reason science has not yet discovered it is that it has not devised the means of doing so.

Why in Ireland?
If we assume the eyewitnesses are reporting genuine creatures in Irish lakes, why are they there in the first place? The identities previously proffered for these lake monsters, including giant eels and primitive whales would have their own unique reasons to account for their presence irrespective of what identity is ultimately shown to be correct.

Take, for example, the giant freshwater eel theory. One of the largest freshwater eels (*Anguilla anguilla*) caught in these islands was an immense specimen by S. Terry in 1971 which weighed 11lbs2oz. As freakish a specimen as this was, it still wouldn't account for the size of some of the creatures reported, assuming they are giant eels.

It has been suggested by various researchers that the reason why a greater proportion of unidentified creatures has been reported during good weather/summer months is due to water stratification resulting in lack of oxygen, thereby forcing creatures to the surface in order to breathe. I would say more people would be about in such weather, hence the observations.

Whenever I started investigating lake monsters, I shared Dr Shuker's impression that primitive whales were seeking out the remote loughs in order to breathe and give birth. However, as so many reports are of single creatures, this might indicate that they do not come to the loughs to breed. Juvenile specimens observed would indicate the horse-eels do not come to the loughs for breeding purposes.

Strange as it may seem, my view is that these creatures enter the Irish loughs in order to drink the fresh water. Monsters seen in impossibly small loughs do not, I feel, dwell there permanently, but move from lough to lough and, indeed, there have been reports of them on land. From studying the isotopic value of archaeocetes' teeth, palaeontologists have deduced that the earliest forms did, indeed, drink fresh water. Research has shown that the earliest archaeocetes such as the pakicetids drank fresh water and even the amphibious Ambulocetus (which is believed to have been marine) needed to stay close to a source of freshwater in order to drink. Any modern evolved forms would have sought this basic necessity.

This would help explain the presence of a large, normally marine-dwelling mammal (albeit of ancient lineage) in a barren, isolated, freshwater lough. In fact Ireland, and especially Connemara, possesses an abundance of lakes – Connemara alone has over 600.

Misidentification of known animals may also provide answers to the identity of the mystery creatures, such as the grey seal. These animals sometimes make their way inland for some unkenned purpose. Perhaps they are looking for Guinness.

Whatever these creatures are, there is one indisputable fact and that is that, in various locations in Ireland, particularly around the west coast, ordinary people are seeing unusual, unidentified animals.

Conclusions and Final Thoughts

Since 1966, whilst researching Irish lake monsters, I have tried to find patterns in eyewitness descriptions or the time of day when a sighting occurred. However, it wasn't until 2006 that I discovered a pattern in several sightings, which happened near Clifden. This pattern was staring me in the face.

To the south-west of Clifden lies a large sheltered bay which has to the east a veritable wilderness of 25 square miles – Roundstone Bog. If we include Mannin Bay – perhaps named after Manannan mac Lir, the ancient Irish sea-god – and the blanket bogland, there have been seven sightings here. (Seven doesn't seem a lot, but considering that there have been 42 sightings then the ratio changes). When I studied the relevant Ordnance Survey map I discovered something fascinating: there is a small lough 200m/1800' to the west of Lough Fadda called Lough Gorranabeast. This translates as "lair of the beast lough". I wonder how long this area was known as a favourite site for lake monsters – very interesting.

One of the problems I encountered when delving into reports was the disparity between people seeing complete unidentified animals and those who only saw a hump. I believe the reason is twofold – firstly, the witnesses haven't seen the animal in its entirety as they haven't watched long enough and secondly perhaps the animal didn't want to show more of itself due to its shy nature and justified caution where humans were concerned.

I often wonder why nobody has come forward with definite proof of a monster and then realised that to see a monster was a rare event in itself.

In fact, due to the very nature of Ireland's Atlantic lowland blanket bogs, the immediate region is sparsely populated and no one would have reason to visit this area unless they farmed or fished. Even then the area is sufficiently large for an archaeocete to go undetected.

When I spoke to local man Coilin Mac Hugh at Lough Gowlaun (wrongly referred to as Lough Crolan) in 2000 he said, "Not many people go to the lakes any more. They have no reason."

As I conclude, I wonder why no sightings have been reported since April 2007 (Lough Muck, Connemara). Personally, I would love for a form of primitive whale to continue to visit Ireland's remote loughs in order to have a drink of freshwater; for visitors I regard them, travelling sometimes overland, not as permanent denizens of the lakes.

It will, I feel take a well organised, sufficiently funded programme of research based on scientific principles which might eventually uncover the truth behind the mystery of Ireland's elusive lake monsters, but it will also require a fair bit of good old Irish serendipity.

At various other lakes around the world such as Ness, Champlain and Okanagan there is the possibility that eyewitnesses have mistaken the unusual phenomenon of seiches (large, energy-laden underwater waves) moving inanimate objects such as tree stumps or logs against the wind on the lake's surface. This previously unrecognised and little studied process is caused by thermodine (a pronounced difference in density between layers of warm and cold water) being tilted due to the change in the prevailing wind. The process is accentuated by the topography of the lake basin with the aforementioned lakes having narrow, steep-sided and very long basins. However, the "underwater waves" phenomenon would not account for the Irish sightings. This is because the loughs are much smaller, making it extremely hard to mistake an inanimate object for a living creature. In fact, the detail reported from the majority of sightings in Connemara and elsewhere in Ireland is astounding. Consequently I am inclined to believe that eyewitnesses in the country are observing large unidentified aquatic creatures and have been for a long time indeed.

The most appropriate final words on Irish lake monsters are from that other pioneer of research within the Emerald Isle – Ted Holiday. In an article for *Ireland of the Welcomes Magazine* Vol. 19, No.2) he states "And one day, good fortune with us, we will capture what the good folk of Connemara call a *horse-eel.*"

2

Of Swinish Things

One of the most famous of mythical animals in Ireland is the Black Pig. This is no ordinary porker. Its origin was magical.

A large but discontinuous earthwork stretches across the southern border of Ulster. It is thought to date from the Iron Age and to have originally had a defensive purpose. This purpose, however, has been forgotten and a curious legend attached to its formation.

It seems that a huge Black Pig charged across the country, unearthing the ditch with its snout. It had originally been a schoolmaster who, by sorcerous arts, changed his pupils into hares and one of them into a hound which in that guise slew his (the hound's) brother. The boys' mother, no mean sorceress herself, changed the schoolmaster into a huge Black Pig and hunters pur-

sued it, right across the southerly borders of Ulster. Eventually they caught up with and killed the brute in Co Sligo. Men marvelled at the huge bristles the corpse boasted. One of them stroked the bristles the wrong way and this caused him to fall into an illness, begging for water. His fellow hunters tried to get it from a nearby well, but the well was magical and it was impossible to bring water from it.

In the Co Cavan area, the story was believed that the Dyke was dug up by the progress of a huge worm.

W.B. Yeats was inclined to associate the myth with a prophecy. In his day there was supposed to be a future Battle of the Valley of the Black Pig where the enemies of Ireland would at last be defeated in a particularly gory encounter.

An article on 27th April, 1918, in the *Irish Times* said that in Kiltrushan (Co Roscommon) two children were claiming they could see a black pig, but nobody else could.

One version of the tale is that there was more than one Black Pig. Having been turned into pigs by the schoolmaster, they had fled to various parts of Ireland. There is a track called the Race of the Black Pig in Co Kildare.

We might find an origin of the Black Pig in the mythological Boar of Formael which was blue-black in colour and lacked ears, a tail and testicles, but had teeth that protruded from his mouth in a way that could scarcely be termed attractive.

The Irish seem to have had a boar god who in Christian times was turned into Torc Triath, king of the boars. In Welsh legend he had a parallel called Twrch Trwyth which was pursued by Arthur and his men in the tale *Culhwch ac Olwen.*

However, these stories of boars may have their origin in an ancient myth, diluted with the passage of time. I have stated elsewhere in this book that Finn mac Cool and his followers, the Fianna, were undoubtedly gods originally, whose status was reduced to heroes of yore once Christianity had supplanted paganism. One of those heroes was a warrior called Diarmaid ua Duibhne. The second part of his name may be a genitive form of Donn, the name of the Irish god of the dead. His first name means 'unenvious'. It is possible he is none other than Donn in human form and that his name originally signified "Donn without jealousy". Another man born at the same time was later changed into the Great Boar of Benbulben (Co Sligo). Diarmaid's life was tied in with this creature, of which it had been prophesied it would kill him. Diarmaid, because of a peculiar custom called a *geis* was forced to elope with Finn's betrothed Gráinne and Finn pursued him, at long last chasing the Great Boar of Ben Bulben towards him and it mortally wounded him. Finn could have saved him, but refrained. We may have here a watered-down version of a widely held Celtic boar-myth, involving the death of the god of the dead, which led to his presiding over the departed. This same myth may lie behind all these stories of strange pigs.

In the romance of the sons of Tuirenn, pigs featured notably. A character turned himself into a pig with a magic wand to avoid attack. The sons of Tuirenn were instructed to procure the skin of the pig of King Tuis, which could cure any wound. The seven pigs of Asal, King of the Golden Pillars, could be killed each night and always would be alive again next day and anyone who ate part of one would be immune to disease. We are not given the pigs' viewpoint on such proceedings.

The pig is a much maligned animal, but, as Dick Chipperfield points out in his book *My Friends the Animals* (1963), pigs are intelligent creatures, but few live long enough to reach their full potential. There was, up to the 19th Century, a special Irish breed of pig that was not only very intelligent, but could actually be trained as a gun dog, I mean gun pig. Alas, this breed was not very fat and therefore not as profitable to raise as foreign swine, which have now displaced it entirely.

There can be little doubt that the pig was the centre of some kind of religious cultus, which medieval literature has distorted, but which has left its mark on the legend and folklore of the country.

An interesting pig fact: the longest English-language place name in Ireland is the district of Muckanaghederdauhaulia (Co Galway). It comes from Irish *Muiceanach idir Dhá Sháile* which means 'the pig marsh between the two salt-water places'.

EDITOR'S NOTE: According to J.E Harting in his book *British Extinct Animals* the wild boar *(S. scrofa)* was common in Ireland until at least the 17th Century, although it is not certain at what stage it became extinct. Interestingly, however, he says that the *"Irish wild boar appears to have been a very diminutive animal".*, although he appears to contradict himself a few paragraphs later when he wrote *"Tusks of Wild Boars dug up in Ireland, according to Thompson, are often of goodly dimensions".*

On an equally important cultural matter it should be pointed out that Captain Pugwash's boat was *The Black Pig.* For those not in the know, the series started in 1950, was created by John Ryan, and never contained the smut attributed to it in urban legends.

Could a walrus have strayed into Co Mayo in April 2008? Though resident in the Arctic, walruses have turned up as vagrants in British and Irish waters

3
chriohser and chriohser...

The inimitable Pap Murphy is a mine of local folklore of the west of Ireland and lives on the Mullet Peninsula, which isn't a peninsula but an island, but presumably once was linked to the land. He is the source of a goodly number of accounts of strange creatures mentioned in this volume. The following story concerns Slievemore (Irish *Sliabh Mor*, the great mountain) which is the tallest mountain on Achill Island. About 1956, a shepherd was traversing its slopes with sheep and sheepdog. Nearby was a large bank of heather forming a kind of hedge. Out of this burst an extraordinary creature, neither beast nor bird, contended the witness, but a fish. In fact, it looked like a very large skate. Now Slievemore stands on the Atlantic coast and its north side faces the sea whose thunderous breakers smash themselves with relentless fury against the cliffs, some of which are a thousand feet tall. The skate-like creature dived over the cliff and the sheepdog dived in pursuit. No doubt the shocked shepherd thought he had seen the last of his faithful hound, but such was not the case. It returned two days later in a woebegone state, covered with blood and not even able to bark. What the strange hedge-frequenting creature was remains a mystery. But the witness remained adamant that it was a fish.

Strange creatures are not confined to the wild. They can turn up in the cowshed as well. In April 2008 a woman from Termon (Co Mayo) went into her cowshed, no doubt expecting to see nothing other than bovine beasts. She saw instead a dark animal, which could have been black or brown, as the light was dimming. She described it as having a very long nose which dragged on the ground, a hump, four legs and a long tail. Its belly seemed to reach the ground. It was accompanied by a younger animal of the same sort. On a further occasion she saw it making its way swiftly towards the shore.

What had she seen? Some of the points of description remind one of the elephant seal – here the big nose comes into play. However, another possible solution occurs to me – perhaps it was a walrus with young. She could have mistaken the tusks, in the twilight, for a long nose.

The appearance of the odd walrus is not unknown in Irish waters – but few of them venture into cowsheds.

A much vaguer creature with few details is reported from Cartron, also in Mayo. A local man was cycling home when he beheld an unidentified creature which he at first mistook for a calf. It roared at him, which must certainly have proved disconcerting. This incident occurred in the 1940s and details of the animal seem unclear. Presumably, it wasn't a member of the local fauna or the cyclist would have recognised it. We are, howver, given no information about the hour or visibility.

Returning to Termon, we find a more recent account of something strange from October or November, 2005. One Cyril Lavelle,then aged about 21, was driving nearby when his head-lights lit up a creature the size of a six-month old calf. It was dark brown or black and its head was large. Its form blocked the road. However, no doubt the beast had a wish to facilitate lo-cal traffic, for it went plunging through a fence. This was no ghostly creature, as the wrecked fence was there for all to see next morning.

If you have a gravid mare who carries her foal for 366 days, the foal which is born will be believed to be a fairy foal, called in Irish *fíor lár*. They rarely occur. I wonder, bearing in mind the length of gestation, whether there is some calendar myth behind this belief. There were horse goddesses in other Celtic cultures, such as the continental Epona and probably also the Welsh Rhiannon. With the advent of Christianity, any such myths seem to have become frag-mented.

A rather mysterious animal seems to have turned up in Clones, Co Monaghan, in 1944. *The Anglo-Celt* of 9th September of that year says Mr George Knight, attorney, took action to deal with a strange animal that was raiding fowl houses (as distinct from foul houses). They set a baited trap for it, but, although it took the bait, it remained uncaptured. It could not be readily identified.

The crane ** (Irish *corr*) has been extinct in Ireland for some time, though its kinsbird, the heron, is still seen. P.W. Joyce, how-ever, quotes a legend that there is a single one on the island of Inishkea (Co Mayo) that has been there since the beginning of the world and will remain there until its end.

** Cranes were breeding burds on mainland Britain until the Sixteenth Century. They were hunted to extinc-tion, and were only rare visitors for the next four hun-dred years until they started breeding in various parts of the country again in the late 20th Century. It is certainly not impossible that a similar situation has occurred in Ireland, effectively bolstering up the old legend. (**Pic: Tina Phillips**)

People have sometimes reported curious lights which behave at times as though they were living beings. Such reports have come in from Britain and the forested Big Thicket area of Texas. I have been able to discover only two cases in Ireland. In the graveyard in Drombeg (Co Down) a glowing ball of light has been seen dancing around. One also rolls around the lake at Crom Castle (Co Fermanagh).

The barnacle goose (*Branta leucopsis*) was the subject of a singular myth in Ireland. It migrated in winter, so nobody saw it breed. The belief grew up that the barnacles that grew on ships turned into barnacle geese. At first their shells protected them, then these were replaced by feathers. This tale spread to Europe and many believed it. The sage scientist Albertus Magnus, however, dismissed it.

We shall be dealing elsewhere with snakes. However, there is in both the United States and Scandinavia a legend that certain snakes will put their tails in their mouths and roll downhill. As Ireland has no snakes, the same story is told of the brown eel (*Anguilla anguilla*). Zoologists tend to scorn the whole idea.

There have been various stories from around the world about birds carrying off children. The golden eagle became extinct or virtually so in Ireland, but it is now being reintroduced in Donegal. However, in Co Mayo the island of Achill, whose very name means 'eagle', used to be home to these birds.

According to Anderson's *Birds of Ireland*, there is an account there of a woman carrying a child who found a fox attacking her chickens. Laying down the child, she attacked the predator, which fled. Then she saw a golden eagle carrying off the child. It carried it off the island. Horror-stricken, she and some men gave chase in a boat, the eagle being just discernable in the distance. It flew to Clare Island, onetime headquarters of Gráinne O'Malley, sea-queen of the Western Isles – which was about five miles distant. The eagle made for its eyrie on a cliffside, where hungry eaglets awaited. From the clifftop, men lowered themselves on ropes to the ledge where the eyrie was located. They found the eaglets tucking into a lamb while the baby was perfectly all right. It seems it was still wearing a red shawl, which was the tradition on Achill Island. Zoologists still deny that a golden eagle could carry off a baby, but surely if one can carry off a lamb, a baby should be possible and their ability to hoist a lamb aloft is not in doubt.

Allusion is made by the lexicographer O'Reilly to a bird named a *geilt*. This word is usually used to mean a lunatic, but obviously has a different meaning here. O'Reilly says it means a fierce bird, species unknown, which cannot be tamed. Forbes says it is more or less mythical.

I have left the last creature in this section to a firsthand account by Louise Donnan. This happened near Kilkeel (Co Down). She and her niece Claire were motoring along, Claire having just passed her driving test. In the distance, they saw an animal on the grass verge of the road. In the distance it looked like a sheep, though it was very big for one. As they neared the creature, they slowed down to have a good look at it. It turned and looked at them. Said Louise, "We both gagged in disbelief and revulsion". Instead of wool, its coat resembled torn rags. It

charged straight at the car, which at this stage was scarcely moving, and put its face up against Claire's window. They looked right into its eye – only one eye was discernable, the other covered by its tatty coat. Both were almost frozen with fear as the eye looking at them was reddish and gave a terrible, wild, penetrating stare. Louise says, "When I looked in its eye I could almost see its mind working powerfully behind it – a mind not of an ordinary animal, but of one with another sense and evil, which I had never encountered before (nor since). I felt sick with fear, but thankfully Claire was able to compose herself and accelerate and took off at an impressive speed. Our relief was very short-lived as we suddenly felt a thud at the side of the car.

To our horror, the 'animal' we thought we had gotten away from was running alongside us and deliberately banging into the car. I screamed at Claire to go faster, which she did, and we both felt terror and disbelief that this thing was able to keep up with us. Just as I felt that we weren't going to get away, the 'animal' suddenly stopped the chase and just stood in the middle of the road watching us escape at great speed. I got the impression that the 'animal' hadn't even tired, but, for whatever reason, had made the decision to go no further, as if it had reached the edge of its 'territory'."

People told the witnesses that all they had seen was a dog, but they were sure this was not the case. Louise was later told by a friend he had heard a few others tell a similar story.

Speaking later to Claire, they shared the following dialogue:-

Claire: That was no dog.
Louise: That was no sheep.
Claire: That was evil.

4

Mythological Monsters

I rish mythology is somewhat difficult to decipher as, with the adoption of Christianity, gods were transformed into heroes who had lived in the past. One such was Fergus mac leide, who may originally have been a god of the Ulstermen, but by historical times was regarded as an ancient king, who had fought a mighty monster in Dundrum Bay (Co Down). This marine inlet was in times agone known as Lough Rudraige.

King Fergus on one occasion captured three leprechauns (*see below for more details*) and offered to let them go on condition they gave him the power to swim under water, which they readily granted, but cautioned him never to swim in Dundrum Bay.

As you may have guessed, this is what the king did. Here he encountered a monster so hideous that its appearance twisted his mouth around onto the side of his face. When he returned to the shore, a problem ensued. No one with a physical blemish could hold the kingship, yet when his courtiers saw the state of Fergus's face, they felt he had acquired a blemish indeed. The king was so popular, however, that his followers resolved that no one would tell him that the blemish existed and this deception lasted for a while. Now, if my mouth were suddenly transferred to the side of my face, I cannot help but think I would notice, whether anyone told me or not. Take the eating question, for example. Surely you'd notice that the mouth into which you were shovelling your

food had changed location? But no, Fergus was deceived until a slave told him. He was furious with the muirdris and determined to kill him.

Around about this time, people seemed to have stopped referring to the beast as the *muirdris* and started calling it the *sinach.* What's in a name? Fergus was determined to slay it, whatever it was called. Into the waters of Dundrum Bay he dived and interested onlookers watched the turbulence of the waters as man and monster contended. At length Fergus emerged with the monster's head, but he himself promptly dropped dead from his wounds.

The question arises concerning what sort of monster the *muirdris* actually was. No description remains. As for its name, the prefix *muir* would indicate it was a sea-monster. At least one writer thought that, because of the name *sinach* came from *sine* (nipple), it must have been mammalian. However, the root of the word is *sín* (weather, with a connotation of bad weather) so it would probably mean something which stirs up the water into a tempestuous frenzy. The word may be related to the words *smeirdris, smergris* which were used to signify some kind of water monster in early times. Howsoever, we can offer no further clue as to the nature of the *muirdris.*

This was not the only mythological monster allegedly slain in prehistoric times. A noted serpent was slain by the hero Fraoch, who was supposedly the son of the goddess Bebinn, while a great number fell by the hand of the celebrated Fionn mac Cumhail (Finn son of Cool), one of the greatest Irish heroes. These, however, were not historical monsters, as Finn was undoubtedly a Celtic god in origin, called *Vindos.* He is remembered in the Continental Celtic name of Vindobona (now Vienna) and in Welsh folklore as Gwyn ap Nudd.

The leprechauns are mentioned above and, though they cannot be classed as mystery animals, they are so well-known outside Ireland that I shall mention them briefly here. Their name derives from *lúchorpán* (small body) and in early times they were regarded as gregarious and possibly aquatic. In modern folklore, the leprechaun is of a solitary nature and is often depicted as a shoemaker.

An interesting kind of monster in Irish mythology was the polycephalid, the creature with more than the usual complement of heads. The most famous of these was perhaps Ellen the Three-Headed, who emerged from a cave in Co Roscommon, but met his end at the hand of the hero Amergin. There was also Garbh of Gleann Ri, to whom Cuchullainn put an end: he had a mere two heads. He was well outdone by Cimbe the Four-Headed. These beings were possibly conceived of as being in human form, apart from in the cranial department.

Leaving straightforward mythology behind us, let us proceed to St Patrick, an undoubtedly historical figure of the 5th Century. Our certain knowledge about him is, however, limited to his own acknowledged writings, the *Confessions* and the *Epistle to Coroticus.* This has not prevented many legends growing up about him, one of which involves a lake monster. This beast was called the Caoránach and had something of a history. Finn mac Cool, mentioned above, had once encountered an evil hag, called the Hag of the Finger. She could be killed only with a silver arrow, which, happily, Finn had about his person. He despatched the loathsome crone and that, you would have thought, was that. Only it wasn't. A hairy worm emerged from the hag's thigh and this grew into a monster, so Finn had to deal with this. He speared it into a vulnerable spot and it went into the lake, its blood giving a reddish coloration to the water. Hence the lake, in Co Donegal, was called Lough Derg, the Red Lake. However, another legend says St Patrick confined it to the lake. There is a Christian pilgrimage to the lake each year, as it contains the celebrated St Patrick's Purgatory. One cannot help thinking it may once have been a pagan site, Christianised by the Church. There is a legendary bird also which dwells there. This is called the Cornu, huge and black, and it is said it was once a demon whom Patrick transformed into a bird. Incidentally, the reader should not confuse this lake with the one of the same name on the River Shannon. The Shannon itself was said to have been carved out by a huge reptile fleeing from St Patrick, but of course it existed long before his time.

St Patrick was not the only saint connected with driving off monsters and it may be that it some way these monsters symbolised or were in some way the cultic objects of pagan religion. At any rate, calling on a saint to deal with them was generally a pretty good plan. At Loch Cime, whose exact location cannot be determined, but which was somewhere in Galway, St Mochua is supposed to have rescued a swimmer in a singular manner. This unhappy fellow had just been swallowed by a monster in the lake, but the saint managed to get the monster to vomit forth his recent snack and, to everyone's delight, the man was still alive. We must also mention the Cata, a monster which dwelt on Scattery Island, in the River Shannon. St Senan, intent on establishing a monastery there, sent the Cata to dwell in another lake. Nor must we forget St Beircheart, who confined a monster to a lake in Tipperary.

Here we might mention another monster, the Brocshee, whose name means 'fairy badger'. By 'fairy' (*sí*) I think we may understand 'monstrous' in a supernatural kind of way, for it seems these creatures were supposed to make formidable adversaries. St MacCreedy encountered one at Inchiquin, it was said, and chained it to the bottom of a lake. Its den was shown to interested persons at Poulnabruckee. Another of these creatures was said to reside in Shandagan Lake in Co Clare. A man named Ned Quinn reported seeing it and that it had eyes the size of lamps.

Nor must we forget the reputation of Lough Bél Dragan, the Lake of the Dragon's Mouth, now known as Lake Muskry in the Galtee Mountains. It was supposed to have been tenanted by a monster in early times. And lastly, there is a curious beast, perhaps a monster, mentioned in the *Táin Bo Cualigne*. This creature may not be monstrous at all, but Cuchullainn is said to have a grip like one. It is called a *griún* and is clearly thought to be a creature whose grip is something to reckon with. The glossator O'Clery avers it means a hedgehog and, while such an animal has strong enough jaws to break your finger (should you be unwise enough to insert it between them), so small a beast can hardly be meant. Its identity, like that of Jack the Ripper, remains a mystery

Perhaps traditions of monsters in Dundrum Bay and Lough Derg have some genuine memories enshrined in them. Who can say? Elsewhere in this volume, you will read of monsters that have been descried in Ireland in modern rather than early times and will see that the mythos of monsters has not faded entirely into the past.

One early monster in Irish myth was the *gaborchend*. There was a population of these. In Modern Irish this would be spelled *gabharcheann*. This means simply 'goathead' and you would think it meant a goat-headed hominid, but in early Irish it could also mean 'horse-head', so what sort of head these creatures were envisaged as having cannot be said with certainty.

From mythology we may perhaps mention one more mythical creature, a lady who rejoiced in the name of Coincheann, which means 'doghead'. The name was hardly inappropriate, as she sported a dog's head. She was eventually slain by Art son of Conn, a king from the mythological prehistoric period.

One of the tales of early Ireland was the *Voyage of Mael Dún*. This tale belonged to a class of stories called *imramma* or voyages in which the hero and a crew would go seawards into the Atlantic and have sundry adventures. On Mael Dún's voyage zoomythological animals he encountered were ants the size of foals; a beast that looked like a horse but had legs like a hound, which seemed eager to dine on them; and a beast that could turn itself around inside its skin, which is a good trick if you can do it. The Atlantic must have been a great thing of mystery to the ancient Irish. They tended to place paradise-like islands there. No doubt the odd artefact of Native American manufacture washed up on the Irish coast, stimulating imagination.

There seems to be a fairly widespread belief that there are horses in the sea, just like those on the land. This seems to stem from a belief that all terrestrial beasts have their marine counterparts. The odd horse with a liking for an occasional swim, spied from the shore, may have added to this idea. However, those horses in the watery domain seem to be conceived in some way different from land horses, though they seem to have the same shape. The reason for this is that one term for them in Irish is *capall nimhe*, which means 'poisonous horse'. This does not necessarily mean the horses concerned are thought of as venomous, but it does indicate they are dangerous.

St Attracta is credited with killing a monster in Co Sligo. It was half-bear, half-dragon. The likelihood of there being an actual beast behind this legend I leave to the reader's judgement. The pseudo-historians of the Middle Ages concocted a legend about a king called Cairbre Cathead (*catcheann*) who overthrew the king of Ireland. This monarch did not feel his feline appendage was enough to exclude him from monarchy and his name has been used to suggest the wildcat was known in early Ireland. In fact, he is a synthetic character and his name does not reflect a genuine tradition. It is probably taken from that of the mythical Cairbre Catutcheann, whose name in this case means 'hard-headed'.

Giants were not probably a feature of Irish mythology, though the Irish pantheon contained two sets of gods, the Tuatha Dé Danaan and the Fomorians. The latter contained Balor of the Evil Eye who may well have been thought of as being of gigantic stature, but perhaps all the gods were. The later tales of Finn mac Cool make him a giant, though Keating inveighs against this. The Irish word for a giant is *fathach* which is derived from *aitheach* (churl) which would indicate that in later legends about giants they were thought of as being no more

THE GIANT'S GRAVE.

than monstrous rustics.

Erard mac Cossi, an historical poet who flourished in the 10th Century, came on a giantess who told him her husband had been killed fighting the fairies and had been buried at Clonmacnoise, a large monastic establishment. In due course the giant's grave was discovered and a dead giant, 15' high, was within. Green birch branches separated the body from the clay. A subsequent excavation of the grave found the branches of green birch, but no body. Unless *gruagach* (see Hairy Hominids) was an early term for a giant, we cannot be in any way optimistic there were large hominids roaming Ireland coeval with modern humans. Incidentally, this giant was not depicted as subhuman. In fact, the poet seemed to take quite a shine to the giantess.

We can combine two mythical creatures in a legend culled from Lickerstown (Co Kilkenny). Here we have a flying horse, though, unlike Pegasus, it appears to be unendowed with wings. Riding it we have a giant called Ceadach. However, for various reasons, I suspect he was originally a god or demon and no flying horse has a prototype which navigated the airways of Co Kilkenny.

I cannot let this section pass without reference to a literary monster called *Liath-charraig*. This is found in a work of the 18th Century called *Lomnochtain an tSléibhe Riffe*. It means 'grey rock'. It is, apparently, none other than the roc or rukh of *The Arabian Nights* in a very strange guise indeed. The writer may have thought the word *roc* was related to English *rock*. Another interesting little snippet concerning a Greek mythical creature comes from Vallency's *Collectanea de Rebus Hibernicus* (1783). In this he assures us that the word centaur is derived from Irish *cean-tar-os* meaning 'chief of sorcerers'. I hasten to add that it isn't.

Appendix

List of monsters (perhaps incomplete) allegedly slain by the hero Fionn mac Cumhail (Finn mac Cool).

A water-serpent; monsters of Lough Neagh, Lough Cuilleann, the Dark Glen, Howth, Erne, Lough Righ, Glenarm, Lough Sileann, Loch Foyle (two), the Shannon, Glen Inne (two), Lough Meilge, Lough Cara, Lough Made, Lough Leaghheia (flame-breathing), Lough Lurga, the River Bann.

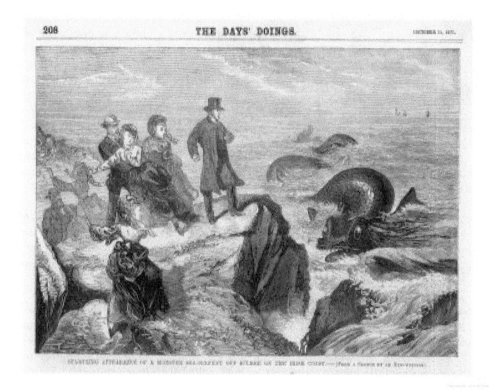

"Sea monster seen by several people off Kilkee, Ireland"

5

Sea-serpents

Perhaps the most famous of all cryptids is the sea-serpent and such creatures have certainly been reported from all parts of the globe. Attempts to classify the various categories of sea-serpent have not met with great success, largely because no undoubted specimens have been examined. Moreover, even supposed eyewitness statements can be so prone to error, they cannot be used as proof positive that such creatures exist, let alone serve as the basis for a classification system. Sea serpents allegedly discovered ashore often turn out to be the remains of basking sharks (*Cetorhinus maximus*), which are called sunfish in Ireland, but should not be confused with the term 'sunfish' of standard English, which is applied to a number of different species.

The early Irish were more than familiar with the concept of strange beasts in the water and several words for such creatures exist, though it must be borne in mind that they could be the product of erroneous observation. The word *bledmell* signified a sea-monster of some kind, as did *cenennan* and *rochuaid*. They also refer to a monster named a *rosualt*, whose name is derived from the Norse word for a walrus, but is not the same thing. In fact, Forbes thinks this was a plague-bearing monster. One is left with the feeling, though, that these could have been anything, including whales. I know of no instance where the Irish word for a serpent (*nathair*) was applied to a sea-monster. Although *piast, peist* (from Latin *bestia*) has been applied to lake monsters, it is also applied to sea-serpents, sometimes in the form *ollpheist*. Lewis Spence says in Scottish Gaelic the term *uilebheist* was applied to a multi-headed monster.

The story of St Brendan includes a mighty whale, so large that the saint and his companions mistook it for an island. This colossus was called Jasconius, whose name is derived from Irish *iasc*, a fish. Of course, this story has been told of other mariners as well. Lough Foyle, an inlet of the sea between Donegal and Derry, is supposedly home to a sort of dragon. This creature was supposed to have ram-like horns, scales and to be venomous. At first, it seems to have been a land animal, if legend is to be believed. However, the locals weren't too happy with its proximity and, St Patrick having recently died, they sent for St Murrough to dispose of it. The dragon informed him that he was going to eat him and St Murrough asked for permission to first put three iron rods on his back. The dragon, who should have known better, agreed to this. Seeing that the reptilian gourmet still regarded him as a forthcoming meal, St Murrough did some hefty praying and the rods formed themselves into a cage around the dragon. St Murrough confined him to Lough Foyle and informed him that there he would rest until the Day of Judgment.

In the Aran Islands there is a blowhole cave which was supposedly occupied by a sea-serpent. This cave is appropriately called the Serpent's Lair.

Lough Swilly, an inlet of the sea in Co Donegal, is supposedly named after the *Súileach*, a many-eyed sea monster that lived in it in the early Middle Ages.

Forbes mentions *badroshan* as an Irish name for a monster, but does not say if it is terrestrial, marine or indeed what it is. As can be seen, the spelling is anglicised.

Having said this, it is time to get on to sea monsters seen off the Irish coast in modern times. The *Cork Reporter* speaks of such an animal discerned in the year 1850. It was observed from a boat by Robert Travers and others, who estimated its length at 30'. It was apparently scratching itself against a beacon. A rifle bullet caused it to leap into the air and crash down into the waters. The *Cork Constitution* in the same year is likely to be reporting the same animal which, it informs us, was seen in the Bay of Kinsale. This serpent was supposedly killed at Youghal. However, H. O'Callaghan, a bank official, states in a letter of 1850 that the story is a hoax, concocted to irritate a man named J.W. Travers, whose namesake was a protagonist.

We are given to understand it was successful in annoying the pants off Mr Travers.

The *Nenagh Guardian* (May 20th, 1950) ran a column of news items from a hundred years before. This tells us that in 1850 two men named Walsh and Hogan reported seeing a sea-serpent or similar beast when sailing between Dundalk and Sutton in Dublin Bay at 6.30 p.m. The creature appeared to be speeding towards Howth and the parts visible looked like coils. The head resembled that of an eel. The witnesses – it is implied that Walsh and Hogan were not the only two – reckoned that the creature was 100' long and was definitely not a whale.

A picture in the Mary Evans Picture Library shows a serpent viewed off Kilkee (Co Clare) in 1871, with several humans regarding it, among them a man who looks as though he takes such creatures in his stride. This seems to be a serpent reported in *Harpers* in the United States, where the witness is described as a clergyman.

In 1907 the chief officer of the *Campania* drew a sea-serpent he had viewed near Cork. This was Sir Arthur Rostron, who later became Cunard commodore. On the 26th April he passed

Cunard Liner, " Campania."

within 50' of the monster and its neck rose eight or nine feet above the water, while it turned its head back and forth, taking a good look at its surroundings. Rostron drew a sketch of it which showed little projections (ears? horns?) at the top of its head. This able officer, who later rescued many of the survivors from the *Titanic*, was quite sure what he had seen was a sea-serpent.

The *Freeman's Journal* (September 11th, 1908) reported that a resident on the Copeland Islands in Belfast Lough (an inlet of the sea) wrote to the *Belfast Newsletter* saying that he and his brother had encountered a sea-monster stranded on the shoal at Horse's Point. He said it had been huge and serpentine. He described the body as being 30' long, covered with scales and endowed with three large fins, two on its back, one underneath. Its circumference was about 6' at its upper fins, but it tapered to 6" round the tail. The mouth, nose and tail looked like those of a conger eel, but were about five times bigger. The witness and his brother used a gun to kill it and, with the aid of two other men and a pony, dragged it ashore. It was beached at Donaghadee (Co Down).

In 1910 a sea-serpent with a brown hairy body and a 6' neck was seen off the coast of Co Galway.

A celebrated but dubious account concerns the sinking of a British ship, the *Iberian*, off the Irish coast during World War I (1914-18). The ship was torpedoed on July 31st, 1915. The captain of the German U-boat (U28), Baron von Forstner (1882-1940) was to say in 1933 that the ship had exploded after sinking, sending debris and a monster shaped somewhat like a crocodile into the air. However, the ship's *Kriegstagebucher* (diary) makes no mention of any monster, nor do any of the survivors from the British ship seem to have spoken of it.

The *Connacht Sentinel* (May 7th, 1935) tells that two fishermen were at the lighthouse on Mutton Island (Co Galway) when they saw a disturbance reminiscent of a small waterspout heading towards them. They headed for Galway instanter. John Crowley, the lighthouse keeper, had also seen the phenomenon and, like the fishermen, was sure it was a sea monster. Two days later, the lighthouse keeper saw the creature again and fired six bullets into its head. The article does not furnish further description.

Hook Head is one of the two capes at the south end of the Barrow estuary in Co Wexford. Here, in 1975, a monster resembling a lizard, about 20' long, was seen by fishermen. At Cahore Point, also in Co Wexford, a long-necked monster was reported. It made worm-like movements. I am doubtful that you could regard the curious animal seen in 1921 in Co Cork by Thady Byrne as a sea-serpent. In fact, one cannot be sure that it emerged from the water at all, but it appeared near a sea-inlet. Details of what Thady observed will be found in Chapter One.

An American newspaper, the *Kingston Daily Freeman* (17th June, 1922) speaks of two Irish sea monsters of which the present writer has not heard. The first is called the Gorramooloch, which looked like a porpoise and was 100' long, reported off Connemara (Co Galway), Mayo and Donegal. It seems to be chiefly nocturnal, with an appetite for gannet. The second, the

Bodree More, is a sea-serpent which Irish fishermen fear will bring bad luck to the observer. I would be inclined to dismiss this pair as the results of journalistic imagination, were it not for the fact that both terms look like genuine English transliterations of Irish words. The Gorramooloch translates back into Irish as *Gormshúileach*, 'the blue-eyed one', while Bodree More would give in Irish *Bodraidhe Mór*, 'the great deaf one'. Neither seems to be regularly seen today.

EDITOR'S NOTE: Writing in his book *Monstrum* (1989) Tony `Doc` Shiels says:

"1983 was the fifteenth anniversary of Nessie's headline-hitting debut, but I devoted most of my monster-raising energies to the Irish creatures.

Some forty-odd miles north-west of Galway town, below Beanna Beola, on the way to Clifden, is a chain of dragon-haunted waters: Lough Leane, Derryclare Lough and Ballynahinch Lake. On a warm mid-September afternoon, as I gazed at Lough Inagh, a small dark hump broke the surface, about a hundred and fifty yards from the shore. I raised my camera and just had time to take one shot before the hump submerged and vanished. Later that day, something guided me towards Maumeen Lough, and up came another hump. Two sightings in one afternoon was incredible, but the incredible had suddenly happened.

Later, on Achill Island, Co. Mayo, I saw another peiste. Achill is quite famous for its water monsters. For at least half a century there have been sightings of a 'huge animal' in Straheens Lough, near Achill Sound, but that particular beast avoided showing itself to me. However, one day, after a lunchtime jar of stout at Keel, Chris, Kate, her boyfriend, and I strolled onto the local golf course, between Trawmore Sound and the south shore of Keel Lough. Whatever impulse had guided us there must have been quite unconscious because we were, all four, taken absolutely by surprise when a smooth, off-white, elongated hump rose gently to the surface and moved slowly eastward though the water. I remember thinking 'this is ridiculous... impossible' as I raised the camera and snapped just one shot before the weird thing submerged It looked rather like the 'forehead' of an albino whale, so I gave it the nickname 'Moby Mick'."

Pl. VII. pag. 180.

LE BLAIREAU.

There is only one species of badger in Europe, the Eurasian badger *(Meles meles)*. But could a second, the `pork badger`, an edible creature no less, once have lived in Ireland?

6

Of ordinary beasts and beasts unknown

T his may seem a rather strange heading for a book that primarily is directed at crypto-zoology, but it does not deal with 'ordinary' ordinary beasts, but rather with animals not native to Ireland that have been introduced into or reported from the country or about which strange beliefs obtain. "Beasts unknown" refers to mysterious beasts which have not been identified.

The Irish cherish some unusual beliefs about the animals of their country. Let us first look at the badger. There is only one species of badger in Ireland, the European (*Meles meles*), but in the belief of the west of Ireland there were two - one edible, the other not. The edible one was called the 'pork badger' and was believed to eat nothing in the wild but vegetable matter. The inedible one was called the dog badger and was not above eating carrion, including bodies dug up from human graves. Just how these two species are to be distinguished I have no notion. I shall refrain from eating badger, just in case.

1919 was the year in which the Irish War of Independence broke out. It was also the year when the *Irish Independent* (11th October, 1919) reported a most curious animal in the vicinity of Drumshambo. Its skin reminded one of a seal, but it had a long snout and was the size of a pig. Rumour had it that there was a chain around its neck. My own suspicion would be that it might have been an aardvark (*Orycteropus afer*), but when hens and geese started disappearing on a nightly basis after its reported appearance, locals blamed it as the culprit. I cannot imagine an aardvark scoffing hens and geese. Their usual diet consists of insects and a strange kind of cucumber (*Cucumis humifructus*). The chain would definitely imply an escaped animal.

In 1924 the *Freeman's Journal* (23rd July, 1924) reported a peculiar animal at Bagnalstown (now called Muine Bheag, Co Carlow). It was supposed to look like half a sheep and half a deer. The report does not say which half looked like which. It was occupying a field with a donkey, with which it seemed on amicable terms.

According to the *Irish Independent* (April 30th, 1926), a bear was apparently shot in Co Monaghan and put on exhibition as "the Newbliss Bear". It turned out to be a badger. Bears have not been found wild in Ireland since BC 1000.

The *Anglo-Celt* (9th January, 1937) reports that when men were hunting about a couple of miles from Arva, an animal that looked somewhat like a badger and somewhat like an otter, but was neither, appeared ahead of them. The hunters killed it. It was said to have had very short legs.

The spider is of course, no stranger to the Irish, but in Clare it was believed there was a special type – the Blood-sucking spider. This could grow to the size of a piglet and it would attack children in the night. Few people have much notion of how many unknown insects there are frolicking about even in their own back gardens, but I think they'd notice the Blood-sucking spider.

Pic: Evan James Hymo

Many Irish people would be surprised by the number of foreign animals that have been introduced into the country. One such is the Bank vole (*Clethrionomys glareolus*). Voles never came to Ireland from Britain, the sea proving a barrier. Then in 1964 the bank vole was spotted for the first time in Listowel (Co Kerry). The assumption was that some had somehow arrived from Britain, but DNA research has now revealed that their ancestors came from Germany. It has been suggested this happened in 1925. In that year the German company Siemens brought earth-moving equipment, still containing soil, into Ireland to build a power station. This was unloaded near Foynes which, as it happens, is near Listowel. By 1982 it was shown that bank voles were to be found in Kerry, Limerick, Clare, Cork and Tipperary. The effect of this introduction has been quite beneficial to the ecosystem. If this seems strange enough, the pygmy shrew (*Sorex minutus*), a recognised Irish animal that probably arrived in prehistoric times, is thought to have made its way hither from Andorra in the Pyrenees, using the obliging transport provided by human-built boats. Presumably they migrated from Andorra (which is landlocked) to the coast of what is now the Basque Country.

Rats do not seem to have been found in Europe prior to the 12th Century, but Giraldus Cambrensis certainly records them in Ireland then. In fact, this is the first time they are recorded in Europe. The rats Giraldus mentions were black rats (*Rattus rattus*). The Irish were well aware of their foreign origin. The Irish for a rat was *luch francach* (French mouse), which was later shortened to simply *francach*. The black rat is scarce in Ireland nowadays, for, in the 17th Century, the brown rat (*Rattus norvegicus*), having migrated from Russia, reached the Baltic Sea. There it found the ideal form of transport: ships. On these vessels it was carried all over the world and, when it reached Ireland, it proceeded to extirpate the black rat. These days, the only places in Ireland you are likely to see a black rat is at the wharfside, where some may have skipped off ships. The two species never interbreed. Even experiments with artificial insemination have failed, the mother reabsorbing the embryos. To confuse matters, brown rats can be black in colour and black rats brown. White rats are actually brown rats.

Rumours started that Ireland harboured rats the size of cats and rabbits and they were said to have eaten a woman and child in Merrion in Dublin in 1729. Rather than this being a gigantic mutant species of rat prowling 18th Century Dublin, however, I suspect the problem here was that of the fact that people who don't often see normal rats can be taken aback by the size. One tends to think of a rat as being like a mouse, only a little larger, whereas you can encounter considerably larger rats and think they are monstrous specimens. In Belfast recently there have been reports that a mutant super rat has developed, 22" long and impervious to poison. City authorities have denied this. I knew a young lady who claimed to have fallen over one, but, as she was in a state of some inebriation at the time, her testimony must be treated with reserve. There are two Irish islands, Tory (Co Donegal) and Inishmurray (Co Sligo) where rats are supposedly unable to dwell due to saintly intercession. An Egyptian subspecies of the house mouse or something that looks very like it has been known in Ireland from 1926.

Before leaving the subject of rats, I feel I should throw in a few words on the subject of "rat whispering", an old Irish custom on which there is an article in *The Irish Monthly*, Volume 53, 1925. Apparently some people seem to have the art of communicating with rats on a premises and asking them to leave it, whereupon they comply. In 1716 the Reverend John O'Mulcrony, descendant of the Irish bards, decided to banish the rats from his graveyard at Kilferagh. He whispered to them and next morning a surprised farmer saw a great horde of rats making their way out of the area. There was a man in Kilkee (Co Clare) who was able to do this in the 19th Century. In what would seem to be a recent instance reported in the article, an Essex farmer was generous to an Irish tramp, who whispered the rats for him and they vacated his farm. He insisted on following the procedure on his own.

It was once believed that the frog was not indigenous to Ireland. Giraldus says it was not to be found there and the appearance of one in the 12th Century caused King Donal of Ossory to prognosticate gloomily. But there must always have been a small number as DNA research at the University of London has shown that the DNA of Irish frogs is different from their British counterparts. This means that the frog population of Ireland that existed before the Ice Age cannot have died out completely, but must have found a warm niche somewhere in that wintry spell, emerging when the good weather returned. Foreign frogs were introduced to the Dublin area about the 18th Century and the two breeds would have mixed.

The wolf was once prolific from Ireland, but wolves were exterminated. Somehow an Arctic wolf managed to get on the loose in 1995 and was shot at Lisnaskea (Co Fermanagh).

The prairie dog (*Cynomys*) is, one must admit, a delightful little creature and an enclosure of them is to be found in Belfast Zoo on Cave Hill. However, the prairie dogs tunnel and I understand that sundry members of the colony have made their way down through the interior of the hill and have been found living wild there. I think we may regard them as an introduced species.

Also introduced has been the American mink (*Lutreola vison*) and the general impression is that this fearsome creature is one we could do without, though it now seems to be established.

The grey squirrel (*Sciurus carolinensis*), of which specimens were set loose in Longford in the 20th Century, is not advantageous to the countryside either. The muskrat (*Ondatra zibethica*) seems to have reached Ireland when a Tipperary farmer bought some from Canada in 1927. They escaped and bred. Their potential danger to the environment was huge and a government campaign was undertaken to remove them. The last was trapped in 1934.

There have, of course, always been isolated exotic animals which, for one reason or another, are to be found stravaging around Ireland. Such a one was the lone raccoon found wandering in Dublin in 1936. Happily, it was found a home in the zoo.

Another introduced animal is the wallaby, of which a small colony exists on Lambay Island off Co Dublin.

Another animal, possibly deliberately introduced, is the greater white-toothed shrew (*Crocidura russuli*) which was discovered in Ireland in 2008. It is usually found in France, Germany and Africa.

With regard to animals that are escapees, the red pandas in Belfast Zoo seem to be adepts at this. One escaped in 1999, the other in 2002. The second found itself averse to the stress of urban life and came back, but the first seems to be still out there. The Cave Hill is wooded and provides a good habitat for such an animal. Red pandas are also called catbears and I think this name suits them better, as otherwise they are likely to become confused with the more well-known giant panda. For those not familiar with them, red pandas look rather like red raccoons and are roughly the size of a badger.

The most populous deer in Ireland, the Sika, only appeared there in 1860, when some were released on the Powerscourt estate. Their place of origin is Japan. There have been various escapes and now Ireland has a population of 20,000. The fallow deer was introduced in the Middle Ages and continues to thrive. The Red deer is the native Irish deer and is also found there. A deer differs from an antelope in that the former sheds its horns (antlers) annually, the latter not at all. (The American pronghorn, which sheds every few years, comes somewhere between the two). Although antelope are not found in Ireland, a nyala antelope (*Tragelaphus angasii*) turned up in Wexford on 13th January, 1997. How it arrived there, none know. Well, I suppose somebody may know, but I don't and neither do the official authorities.

Of course, there have always been reports of animals wandering the countryside of nature unkenned. The *Nenagh Guardian* (February 16th, 1898) reports an animal from Roscommon that looked like a pig but was bigger and bore a red shaggy coat. It seems to have taken up residence on the farm of a Mr Bennett of Derrylahan. Two dogs were set on it, but it terrified them and they headed for home, refusing food until the next day. I know nothing of its capture.

The *Killeshadra News* (20th March, 1954) tells of one James Leddy who, when ploughing, found the remains of an animal with "elk-like horns". This doesn't tell us very much as many people have only a vague idea of what an elk is. In Europe the term is used for the moose, in America for the wapiti.

Slieve Russell Mountain, near to Ballymaconell (Co Cavan) was, we are informed by the *Anglo-Celt* (2nd May, 1896), the scene of the discovery of a dead animal which no one could identify. It was almost the size of a donkey, its hair was grey, it had a pig-like head, small eyes and a bushy tail. It had three horny toes on each foot. Although seen by hundreds of people, none volunteered to say what it was.

In 1957 an unidentified but poisoned animal was found by C. O'Leary at Dauros, Kenmare (Co Cork). No other details are provided.

The slow worm or blindworm (*Anguis fragilis*) is neither slow, blind nor a worm, but a legless lizard. It is not supposed to be part of the Irish fauna, but there is now evidence of an introduction by humans in the west. Rumour has it they were introduced in about 1960.

The dace is not a native Irish fish. An English angler introduced the species into the Blackwater River in Cork in 1889.

Snakes have never been in Ireland (unless you count a pre-Ice Age possibility), due to the fact that they did not fancy swimming across from Britain. (The only other European lands from which they are absent are Greenland and Iceland, also due to the water barrier). There is, of course, the famous story that they were banished by St Patrick. He makes no mention of this, however, in his *Confessio*. The occasional one has turned up, either a traveller on a foreign ship who came ashore or an escaped pet. The *Irish Independent* (9th July, 1906) mentions one that was found in a garden at Ranelagh in Dublin. The same newspaper mentions a 30" long in a garden in Merrion Square, Dublin, in its issue of 29th October, 1930. In the same year the *Meath Chronicle* (26th July, 1930) tells us that Mr Charles Murrell was swimming in the Inny when he stepped on what he thought was an eel. It wasn't, it was a snake, and this scion of the house of Murrell required medical attention. On the date of the report, he had almost recovered. Underneath the account is an advertisement making the claim that Winstanley's Irish-made Boots are Wonderful Value. (I put that in just in case you wanted to know). In the previous year, Constable McKaney discovered an 18" snake in Dee Street, Belfast.

If we gaze at the pages of the *Meath Chronicle* (30th June, 1934) we find that Mr C. Daly, who appears to have been a publican, shopkeeper or combination of both, was startled to be told there was a snake on his doorstep. Mr Daly approached, mallet in hand, and took the snake outside, while it made a noise like a gander. Mr Daly walloped the snake on the head thoroughly and flattened it. The snake was found to be 27" long. At some stage the idea seems to have arisen that it was a cobra. The village of Dunshaughlin, scene of these events, was crowded that day due to an election and many came to see the serpentine wonder. A bus passenger who had been abroad in a land where snakes abounded, said he knew this kind of snake and it was no good hitting them on the head, because you couldn't kill them that way. When a journalist arrived, it began to wriggle around, though held in the hands of a man with the auspicious name of Tugwell. The snake was described as multi-coloured. There is no word on its ultimate fate.

Ammonites are an extinct group of marine cephalopods related to octopuses and squids. They became extinct 65 million years ago in the same KT Extinction Event that killed off non-avian dinosaurs. They are, however, well known as fossils.

In medieval Europe, fossilised ammonites were thought to be petrified snakes, and were called "snakestones" or, more commonly in medieval England, "serpentstones".

They were taken to be evidence for the actions of saints such as Saint Hilda and Saint Patrick. Traders would occasionally carve the face of a snake into the empty, wide end of the ammonite fossil and sell them to the public.

The *Irish Times* (22nd July, 2006) contained advice on how to deal with an escaped pet snake, should you encounter one.

The *Kerryman* (1st June, 2006) draws our attention to a mystery animal seen in the vicinity of Knocknagosher. It was seen by one Ritchie Walsh in his back garden. Luke Keane proclaimed it was dark, short-tailed and square-faced He assured reporter Deirdre Walsh that it was not a cat, dog, mink, badger or fox.

An earlier report of a strange animal is to be found in the *Anglo-Celt* (July 22nd, 1939). This is a Cavan paper. A pair of cyclists reported seeing an animal on the Black Lion Road. The body was long and thin, the ears like a rabbit and it had a lengthy bushy tail. Its colour was reddish.

Thomastown (Co Kilkenny) saw the discovery of a group of unidentified animals in a cave around 1780. They looked like boars, but appeared to have antlers or spreading horns. Perhaps these were the results of some cranial disease, but no further information on these creatures seems available.

Around the year 1869 a strange beast was discovered in the vicinity of Slane. It was about the size of a cat, but its face looked like a weasel. The weasel (*Mustela nivalis*) is not found in Ireland, but the term 'weasel' is often applied there to the stoat (*Mustela erminea*). However, this creature was tusked. It had four tusks, two going upward and two down. It had a small mane and twelve toes or claws on each foot. It was captured in a rabbit trap.

Speaking of stoats, it now seems possible there are two races of Irish stoat rather than, as hitherto supposed, one. The Irish stoat (*Mustela erminea hibernica*) is a separate subspecies and may have been in Ireland before the last Ice Age and survived the rigours of that epoch by living under the snow. Some aver that it never turns white in winter, but it is possible there is the odd exception. Stoats are miscalled weasels in Ireland. This may have been caused by the large number of Irish names for the stoat.

Rabbits are not native to Ireland. The Irish word for a rabbit, *coinín*, is derived from English *coney*. Still, they have certainly been here since about 1200, introduced by the Normans. These may also have introduced the hedgehog, for they liked to eat hedgehog. The Irish called this animal *grainneog*, 'little ugly one', which seems somewhat unpleasant.

The red fox (*Vulpes vulpes*) is widely known in Ireland. A black variant turns up in the United States, but it must have appeared occasionally in Ireland for the *Lecan Glossary* gives us the word *fuinche* which it says means a black fox.

There was supposed to have been a race of pigs of giant size in Ireland once. The last place you could find them was Imokilly (Co Cork). One of the Fitzgerald family killed the last of them. Its body began to rot and became a health hazard, causing an outbreak of some illness, so it was thought wise to bury it in a chest.

A rather uncertain animal mentioned in early literature is the *togán* or *togmall* which seem to be different names for the same animal. The legendary Queen Maeve is connected with both. Dinneen, author of a modern dictionary, suggests it belongs to the polecat family, but polecats are unknown in Ireland. However, de Bhaldraithe's modern English-Irish Dictionary, while giving *pólchat* for polecat, gives *toghán* for fitchew which is a synoym. I suspect the animal is in fact a pine-marten rather than some mysterious creature that has vanished from the Irish scene. Forbes, interestingly, gives *tachan, taghan* as meaning both polecat and pine-marten. He suggests *toghmall* means a squirrel and he may indeed by right.

A new kind of butterfly was discovered in Ireland in 2001. It resembles the Wood White in most particulars, but the two do not interbreed. It is known scientifically as *Leptidea reali* and in English as Real's white butterfly. [**]

Global warming has resulted in the arrival of various new species in Ireland. They are known animals and their provenance is in no way mysterious, but I will just mention that they include the Chinese mitten crab, the grey triggerfish, the slipper lobster, the collared dove, the cattle egret and the blackcap. Even a mourning dove, of American origin, has been espied on Inishboffin off the western Irish coast.

Finally, a truly unknown animal, the *tairnill*. It is mentioned in early literature, but, as nobody knows what the word means, its identity remains a thing of mystery.

[**] In an unpublished discussion with Tony `Doc` Shiels, author and lepidopterist Jonathan Downes proposed another new species of Irish butterfly: The Terrible Beauty. It has a difficult transition from caterpillarhood, is green, white and orange in colour and is seen "wherever green is worn".

APPENDIX: THE IRISH STOAT

(Originally published in *The Smaller Mystery Carnivores of the Westcountry* by Jonathan Downes (CFZ, 1996)

It is generally agreed that the Stoat (*Mustela erminea*) is found all over the British Isles, and unlike the Weasel (or probably the Polecat, although this is uncertain) is found in Ireland. Some reports, however, refer to a separate species, the Irish Stoat (*Mustela hibernica*) and it is interesting to note that there seem to be several different opinions as to what exactly it is, and if in fact, it exists.

It is unclear whether or not it is believed that both the 'normal' species of Stoat and the 'Irish' variety co-exist in Ireland, or whether or not only the disputed species is found. Sleeman (1989). [5] refers to an animal the size of an ordinary Weasel (Irish Stoats are often referred to as 'weasels' although true Weasels are confined to the mainland) on which the dividing line between the reddish upper parts and the white belly is much less well defined than on the mainland animal.
Praeger, [6] in 1950, wrote:

> *"The Irish Stoat (Mustela hibernica) is now considered a different species from that found in Britain, on account of its smaller size and darker colour with less 'whitish' underneath; the lips and rims of the ears are dark, while in the English Stoat they are light-coloured. Also the white winter coat, assumed by the animal in the colder parts of the range, and frequently in Britain, is scarcely ever seen.*
>
> *'Common as the animal is in Ireland' writes Thompson, 'I have never seen or heard of a white one being taken in winter. Towards the end of our most severe winters in the north, I never saw any change of fur in these animals. Yet, in the part of Scotland closest to Ireland, where the difference of climate from that on the opposite coast must be most trivial, the stoat becomes white every winter'. This active and daring little animal is common throughout Ireland, where it is usually called 'weasel' (which is 'Mustela nivalis'), and is sometimes also mistaken for the Polecat (Mustela putorius); but neither of these relations of the Stoat is found in Ireland. It is interesting to note that the Isle of Man is colonised by the Irish, not the English Stoat (Mustela erminea stabilis)".*

Moffat [7] also confirms that Irish Stoats are known as 'weasels'. There is some confusion here because he seems to refer to the Irish Stoat as being distinct only at a sub-specific level, although other references cited are convinced that it is a distinct species.

Praeger refers several times to Thompson's classic 1856 work on *Irish Natural History*, [8] but elsewhere Thompson and others [9] collect a few records of the white winter colouration, which suggests that this variety of Stoat, whether or not it is distinct at a specific level, is less prone to this mode of protective colouration than is its English counterpart. This is valuable corroborative evidence for a degree of speciation.

Thompson's book also, incidentally, contains the original reference to the Antrim Beech Marten specimen referred to in the main text of this book, but Thompson seems to suggest that the Beech Marten is by far the rarest of the two Marten species living in Ireland.

The final record we have of the Irish Stoat is so different that, again, it appears to refer to another animal altogether. Scharff (1922) writes: [10]

> "Related to the Marten is the Irish Stoat (Easog), commonly called 'Weasel' in Ireland, an animal quite distinct from the British Stoat, and even more so from the true Weasel. It is unknown outside Ireland, and is much larger than the Weasel. It differs from the English Stoat in having the ears and upper lip dark in colour, and in so far as it rarely turns quite white in winter".

We, therefore, have a Weasel-sized animal with Stoat colouration, a dark, Stoat-sized animal that may or may not turn white in the winter, and an animal half-way between the Weasel and the Stoat in size, which sometimes turns white in winter, but sometimes doesn't.

When you also consider the mystery of the Antrim Beech Marten and the disputed question of whether or not there is an indigenous population of Polecats, the only thing that remains clear is that there is a lot of work still to be done regarding the precise speciation of the Irish mustelidae.

Other references to the Irish Stoat occur in *The Irish Naturalists Journal* Volume 1, numbers 8 (p. 150 – 1), 11 (p. 219 and p. 271), Volume 2, (p. 44 and 73), and Volume 4 (p. 64

REFERENCES

5. SLEEMAN P *Stoats and Weasels, Polecats and Martens* (1989).
6. PRAEGER R.L. *Natural History of Ireland* p.73 (1950).
7. MOFFAT C.B. *The Mammals of Ireland* (*Proceedings of the Royal Irish Academy* Vol. 44 (b) p. 61 – 128. (1938).
8. THOMPSON W. *The Natural History of Ireland* (4 Vols, Bohn, London 1856).
9. *The Irish Naturalist* (March 1895).
10. SCHARFF R.F. *Guide to the collection of Irish Animals.* (Dublin, Stationers Office; 1922).

7

Werewolves and other transformations

I was informed by a letter from the Irish Folklore Commission that there was no tradition of lycanthropy in Ireland. Lycanthropy means a human changing into a wolf or, by extension, some other animal. I find that hard to believe, as I have discovered two native Irish terms for a werewolf. The first is *conriocht*. The second, to be found in Kuno Meyer's *Contributions to Irish Lexicography* (1913) is *conoel*, which in Modern Irish would be spelled *conaol* , and it means specifically a female werewolf.

An early werewolf story set in Ireland is narrated by Giraldus Cambrensis, who came with the Norman Invasion of 1169. He says that about 1163 a priest and a young boy found themselves by night in a wood. A wolf approached them and conversed in human speech. He said there were two of them who had been cursed by Saint Natalis and every seven years they were turned into wolves. At the end of seven years they returned to humanity and two others replaced them. His partner was now dying and needed the last rites of the Church, which the priest administered to her, first tearing off the wolfskin to find an old woman beneath. The male wolf stayed with the travellers overnight and in the morning led them out of the wood.

In the vicinity of Co Kilkenny in early times lived the Osraige. The Osraige were supposed to leave their human bodies from time to time and go about in the shape of wolves. If you happened to touch the human body when one was out wolfing, he would die. If they were killed as wolves, their human bodies would die. Why they should be connected with wolves is a mystery, as the first element in the tribal name is *os*, 'deer'. It has been suggested that it is because one of their supposed ancestors was called Laighneach Wolflike. It is also by no means impossible that, in early times, the men of Ossory wore wolfskins when hunting or in rituals with relation to the hunting of deer.

It would be surprising if there were no werewolf traditions in Ireland, for wolves were once very prolific in the country. In Tudor times, the land was sniving with them and Shakespeare alludes to them. Cromwell started a campaign against them and, some time in the 18th Century, the last Irish wolf breathed his last. There is some dispute about where this occurred.

Elliott O'Donnell, who has written much on ghosts, says many Irish families have werewolf

traditions, but he does not favour us with any examples. In 1874 a strange animal appeared in Limerick. It was described as "wolflike" and went about sinking its teeth into its victims, some of whom later went insane. In the same year in Cavan a mystery animal known as the Cavan Bloodsucker attacked sheep. It drank their blood, but left the carcases virtually untouched. It was also supposed to have attacked people, but descriptions are not to hand.

Wolves weren't the only creatures into which a human could change. Witches were supposed to have the power to change themselves into hares. The hare, perhaps because of the leaping ritual associated with it, has always been regarded as a somewhat strange animal. The normal Irish word for a hare is *giorria* (<*geirrfhiadh*, 'little deer'), but other names have been applied to it – *míol gearr, míol má, míol buí, pata, lornán* - and the Irish hare is a subspecies, *Lepus timidus hibernicus,* of the Arctic hare. The Brown hare (*Lepus capensis*), the species found in Britain, has been introduced to Ireland by humans. Lady Gregory gives two accounts of women who were supposedly were-hares. In one, she was told by Stephen O'Mara, a resident of Connemara, that he had shot a hare that had then changed into a woman. Another man told her that his uncle and a companion chased a hare that made for a house and the greyhound snapped its leg. When they entered the house, they found no hare, but an old woman bleeding.

Hares were generally regarded as being somewhat magical. One man's father had claimed to have seen a procession of a dozen hares on one occasion, walking in Indian file. Another man claimed to have seen a large number of hares proceeding through the night and he was sure they were not hares in reality. A supernatural hare was supposed to be white and would lead the hunt across water into another world. This gave Lewis Carroll the idea for the White Rabbit.

The strangest such animal I have come on in Lady Gregory's writings was a were-eel – a woman with the power to turn herself into an eel. A woman had taught her how to do this, but the effort made her take to her bed afterwards. Sir Martin O'Neill was said to have got her into a room and made her effect the transformation. She complied and he was terrified. He tried to get out, but she placed herself between him and the door, bared her teeth and growled.

A final piece of lore regarding animals that Lady Gregory acquired and which the reader might find interesting was the belief that stoats were serpents in disguise and cats, which do not seem to have been popular amongst the Irish countryfolk, had been serpents once. Stoats (which are often miscalled weasels in Ireland) can sometimes be old witches, we are informed by Lady Wilde (Oscar's mother).

There seems to be a folk belief that only women can change themselves into other creatures.

The occasional story in which the change to animal form is involuntary arises. Erard Mac Cossi, who flourished in the 10th Century and who seems to have been the focus of a number of stories, is involved in one such. He was the chief poet of King Fergal of Connacht. I should mention that the word poet here translates Irish *file* (2 syllables) and that the *file* was to some extent almost a successor to the druids. They were historians, genealogists and wonderworkers in Irish belief and the origin of the word is Celtic **velitas* 'seer'. They were much more than mere poets and Edmond Spenser, in speaking of them, calls them not poets, but, more accurately, 'men of art'. This Erard threw a stone into a flock of swans on one occasion, striking one upon the wing, while the others flew away. Perhaps regretting what he had done, he ran over to his victim, only to discover she was now no swan but a woman. She said the other swans had been demons, who had turned her into a swan when she was sick. The blow from the stone had restored her to humanity. We might mention here the Swan Maiden of Lake Inchiquin (Clare) who married a human.

8

Hybrids

There is a number of accounts of unusual hybrids in Ireland. I myself remember encountering in the village of Duncannon (Co Wexford), as a child, a large animal, hairy and shaggy, which locals said was a cross between a sheep and a goat. Such a cross is not impossible, but I suspect it was merely a goat with distinctly atavistic characteristics. It was known locally as the *Pocán*, which is the Irish name for a male goat, but it was said it had sheep's eyes. I can assure the reader, however, that it had goat's horns, with which it once chased me into a hut; but that is another story.

In the 12th Century, the Normans invaded Ireland and with them came their chronicler, Giraldus Cambrensis. He felt that there were hybrids involving humans and cattle to be found in the country. He mentioned one such creature in Wicklow that looked generally human, but had hooves. He also had a bald head, big eyes and no nose – just a brace of holes in his face that fulfilled the function of nostrils. This unfortunate being was eventually killed.

He also tells of a cow that gave birth to a strange creature in Glendalough, also in Co Wicklow. This creature was supposed to have had a human father and in due course to have developed more like a human than a cow, so he was accepted into human society.

One of the strangest hybrids in Irish legend is the Beast of Lettir Dallan. It is found in the medieval Irish Triads. A priest's daughter (this was before the days of clerical celibacy) was wandering near Glencar Lough near Sligo, when she beheld an *each uisce*, the general term for a lake monster. Taken by its captivating personality, she was seduced by it and gave birth to a monstrous being. This creature had a human head and a body that resembled a set of bellows. There was an ox in the same area called the Ox of Dil, whose father was an *each uisce* and whose mother was a cow.

David Thompson relates the folk legend of *King Cormac and King Conn*, which he heard in Ireland. In this, King Cormac's daughter was made pregnant by an otter. The offspring of this union, however, seemed perfectly human. The only drawback was he couldn't sleep. Otters were believed in the Irish countryside to be perpetually awake.

There is a belief in Co Clare that cats and rabbits will hybridise, but this belief is found in various countries, where such creatures are called such things as *cabbits* and *racats*.

A cat can actually be born with a genetic disorder which makes its hindquarters look like those of a rabbit and in this we may have the origin of this belief.

The people of Clare, at least in days gone by, used to believe you could find from time to time the hybrid of a rook and a hen.

The Irish countryfolk in some places believe it is possible for the hare and rabbit to cross.

Of course, science teaches us that beasts of different genera should not be able to hybridise. However, this is not an invariable rule, so don't become too familiar with any cows or water monsters you might encounter.

9
Lady Gregory's Zoo

Augusta Gregory was one of Ireland's most well-known folklorists and much involved with W.B. Yeats. She lived in Sligo and visited the peasants of the area, collecting their folk-beliefs. Because she spoke Irish fluently, this posed no problem for her. Much of the information she gathered concerned animals. Some even concerned invisible animals.

One of these concerned a servant who lived in an establishment between Waterford and Tramore, where he slept in a room above the stable. He was troubled by night by something lying on top of him and breathing heavily. This sounds like a case of sleep paralysis, but it certainly frightened him, so he kept the fire in his room ablaze at night to make sure the whole place was well lit. He also had a terrier in the room. One night the terrier jumped up and began to fight what seemed to be an invisible opponent. Although the affrighted man could not make out the dog's adversary, his attention was directed to the shadows on the wall. He saw the shadow of the dog fighting the shadow of an invisible creature with a head like a pike's. This creature was about 2' long. After a while the fight stopped, but the terrier would not sleep in the room again.

Two youths, walking along, on one occasion

heard a groaning sound coming from the far side of a wall. One determined to look over it. Walking between two trees he saw a humanoid figure, walking back and forth like a sentry. It was wearing a black suit. The extraordinary thing was that it had the head of a bear. The plucky youth addressed him, but the creature said, "Don't speak to me, don't speak to me." Lady Gregory spoke directly to the youth concerned.

Another piece of direct information came from a man who had been transporting turf along the road. A strange creature emerged from the gutter and stood over him like an elephant. The beast disappeared, but was seen again by the turfman shortly afterwards on his journey. Unfortunately, no clearer description has been preserved. The elephant comparison indicates the creature was large.

Another informant returning home kept running into what he took to be a local donkey by the name of Neddy. Neddy kept getting in his way until at length he heard laughter and realised it was a fairy in disguise.

Returning to the servant who worked between Waterford and Tramore, he said there was once in that area a woman who claimed to have seen a living woolpack, which was propelling itself under its own steam.

Lady Gregory was also told of gigantic worms. One attacked a woman near Clough. It was nearly 8' long.

In addition to the above, Lady Gregory heard tales of strange dogs, of which we will treat in the chapter devoted to such animals. She was also told of women with the ability to turn themselves into other creatures.

10

The wildcat

The wildcat is a difficult animal to research in Ireland, for the term *wildcat* (Irish *fia-chat*) is generally used to mean merely a feral domestic and, if a zoologist is writing in Irish, he will use the term *cat fiain* for the genuine wildcat (*Felis silvestris*), which, according to received wisdom, is not to be found in Ireland. Moreover, the term *wildcat* should not be used of the Alien Big Cats (ABCs) such as pumas and black pan-

PLATE VIII

WILD CAT

thers, reported in the wild from time to time by the media.

However, it has been argued that there are, or at least were, genuine wildcats in Ireland. There is a surprising amount of anecdotal and perhaps archaeological evidence to suggest that an aggressive feline predator has been active for some time.

Intriguingly, I came across a reference to wildcats in Ireland in Michael Viney's authoritative work on the natural and geological history of the country. Simply entitled *Ireland*, on page 58 he states:

> brown bear and wolf were among the country's early predators
> and three more – fox, badger....and wildcat (Felis sylvestris) were
> present by the Neolithic, when people had begun to farm.

He also suggest a possible reason for their (the wildcats') presence: on page 59 he notes

> otter, pine marten, red squirrel – even the wildcat – are all candi-
> dates for early introduction to Ireland for their skins.

For relatively recent reports of wildcats in Ireland, there are several mentioned by Karl Shuker within his *Mystery Cats of the World*. He states within *Notes on the Irish Mammalia* by the once renowned Irish naturalist William Thompson there is an anecdotal account concerning wildcats. Shuker writes

> Having noted on several occasions grouse feathers strewn near a
> water break in his Irish beat, as well as a number of grouse corpses
> beheaded, but otherwise undamaged, the gamekeeper responsible
> for that area set a trap and caught to specimens of what appeared
> to be genuine wildcats, one adult and one juvenile.

Shuker goes on to say that Thompson

> had taken a particular interest in reports of alleged wildcat sightings
> in Ireland, notably in Erris in the county of Mayo.

Indeed, it was from this county that I came upon several reports of wildcats which had been previously undocumented, but more of those later.

Also within *Mystery Cats of the World* , Shuker notes that Thompson

> had also seen a very large cat weighing 10 lbs 9 0z (4.75kg) which
> had been shot at Shane's Castle Park, Co Antrim.

A very intriguing detail concerning this particular account is the cat was very similar to the European wildcat, with the exception of its tail – it was not bushy at the tip. This seemingly mundane point (if you'll excuse the pun) will be discussed in more detail in a later part of this article.

Whilst researching, I consulted *Early Evidence for Wild Animals in Ireland* by Finbar McCormick. Within his paper McCormick states that the wildcat became extinct during the late Bronze Age and Iron Age. Intriguingly, he also quotes R. Warren in *The Irish Naturalist* 14 (1905):

> *There is no doubt that the domestic cat when wild for several generations grows to abnormal size and strength.*

Warren also states that he had shot old males that were

> *twice the size and weight of the house cat which, with same discoloration and markings, only for his pointed tail would have been mistaken for a true 'wildcat'.*

The Great Debate

Indeed there was great intellectual dispute amongst the naturalists of the 19th Century with regard to a genuine form of Irish wildcat. Not only did William Thompson (who was a pioneering naturalist from Belfast) believe in the existence of the wildcat, but so too did the Reverend J.G. Wood, who mentioned it in his Illustrated Natural History series.

At one stage it looked as though only a bona fide specimen would prove the wildcat's existence; and, in fact, this seemed to have occurred in 1885. A.W.B. Tegetmeier presented the skin of an alleged wildcat from Co Donegal at a meeting of the Zoological Society of London. He also allowed Dr E. Hamilton to examine it and consequently it was demonstrated to have been simply a feral domestic.

If the above instance seemingly sounded the death-knell of a possible Irish wildcat events were to take an interesting twist. A paper entitled *The Former Occurrence of the African Wildcat {*Felis ochreata Gmel*) in Ireland* (1906) written by Dr R.F. Scharff concerned itself with his findings after excavating remains found in Eden Vale and Newhall caves near Ennis (Co Clare). Scharff had discovered bones of two distinct breeds of cat, one smaller than the other – the larger of which he attributed to a genuine Irish wildcat, which, he concluded, was closely related to the African wildcat. He arrived at this conclusion after carefully measuring the skulls, jaws and teeth of several specimens and comparing them with other fossilised cats, including mummified Egyptian cats. The findings of Dr Scharff were subsequently challenged by A.W. Stelfox who presented his views in a paper – "Notes on the Irish Wildcat" – published in the *Irish Naturalist* (Volume 15, July, 1965). Stelfox gave a very different opinion – they were simply the male and female of the domestic cat (the larger male, the smaller female). Interestingly, Dr Darren Naish has informed me that the remains found in the caves have now been conclusively identified as the European wildcat (*Felis sylvestris*), thus confirming the belief that Ireland had a genuine form of wildcat.

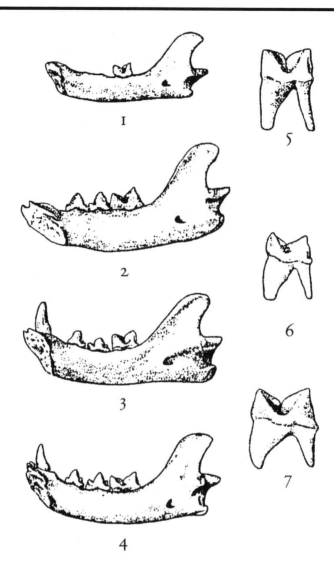

Comparison of jaw-bones found in Newhall Caves, Ireland with those taken from other cats – after R.F.Scharfe (1906).

1. Right ramus of the lower jaw of dwarf form of Domestic Cat *(F.catus)* from Newhall caves.
2. Right ramus of the lower jaw of African Wildcat *(F.lybica)* from Newhall caves.
3. Right ramus of the lower jaw of European Wildcat *(F.silvestris)* from Inverness, Scotland.
4. Right ramus of the lower jaw of African Mummy Cat *(F.lybica)* from Egyptian tomb.
5. Lower carnassial tooth of European Wildcat *(F.silvestris)* from Inverness, Scotland.
6. Lower carnassial tooth of Domestic Cat *(F.catus)* from Cappagh, Co. Waterford.
7. Lower carnassial tooth of African Wildcat *(F.lybica)* from Newhall Caves.

NOTE: The roots of the teeth in figs. 6 and 7 should be twisted more to the right in order to give an exact idea of their position in the alveoli.

Shuker refers to William Hamilton Maxwell's book *Wild Sports of the West* in which are contained several accounts of wildcats.. Along with the tale recounted in Shuker's work there is also that of a male and female wildcat with young. They had been living in a den along the coast which was overrun by rabbits. They were very similar in size and colour to the animal killed by the fox catcher noted in Shuker's work. Maxwell comments that if wildcats were left to their own devices then, in a relatively short time, all the rabbit population would have vanished.

Intriguingly Maxwell goes on to sate that not only is there a large and ferocious species along the coast, but that the "cat becoming wild" also occurs here: Maxwell thus distinguishes clearly between the feral cat and the wildcat.

An interesting point that is noted within Maxwell's relevant chapter dealing with the belief that a bite from such an animal is venomous. This notion is noted in Ballycroy (co Mayo). It may be that people suffered tetanus from a bite. It may also be that the Irish word *nimhe*, while technically meaning venomous can also be used to mean sharp, fierce.

Incredible as it seems, there are several accounts which describe the wildcat's possessing a sharp metallic object at the end of its tail – which has been various labelled a spike, claw or nail.

With T.J. Westropp's *Folklore of County Clare* there is a brief mention of a wildcat. In the chapter "Animal and Plant Superstitions" p. 62, is the reference

> *The wildcat is believed to have a spike or hook on the end of its tail which it can stick into a pursuer, but I found no such fine legend in Clare on this point as I did near Kenry in Limerick, where the cats pursued and anchored themselves onto a farmer and his dog, after chasing them from Clorane to Old Kidimo.*

Of Fangs and Claws

Whilst researching sightings of animals in Ireland's lakes, I corresponded with a man from one of the most isolated and, it must be said, most beautiful regions in Ireland. The Mullet in north-west Co Mayo looks similar to a peninsula jutting out into the Atlantic like an arthritic finger, but it is technically an island, which means that it is Ireland's second largest offshore island after Achill. Pap Murphy is a truly fascinating man in a country full of great characters and fascinating men, yet his knowledge of Co Mayo is humbling. From archaeology to history to folklore, anybody researching this region of Ireland should definitely visit him or his visit will be a complete waste of time.

Pap had often heard of the wildcat, and when questioned told me of an incident which happened around 1940 or 1950. Pap's uncle and father encountered a wildcat in a shed at the end of Pap's uncle's house. According to Pap, the animal was entangled in some fishing nets and debris. It was subsequently killed. The cat was quite large and had growled at both men. The two men also told of the animal's possessing a nail at the end of its tail. When questioned about this very curious physical feature, Pap was adamant it was very sharp and possibly bony – it was not an illusion creating with the tail hairs' ending in a poisoned tip, as I cautiously suggested.

I also learned from Pap that the wildcat was seen on a sandbank at Annaghhead. The area is located west of the town of Belmullet and south of Eagle Island. Apparently the animal possessed the unbelievable ability to elongate its neck.

There are also reports of Irish wildcats in a region very famous for its lake moster sightings, Connemara (Co Galway). Whilst conducting research here in May, 2003, I was told by an elderly man named Francie Burke (he was about 80 when I spoke to him) of the wildcat. He assured me that it was bigger than the ordinary cat and was to be found mostly in wooded areas. Although this western region of Ireland can claim to be a veritable hotspoy of lake monsters, there is a sparsity of reports pertaining to mystery wildcats.

However, one very notable account occurred in the immediate environs of Lough Narawaun. (This lake is often quoted as Lough Nahooin in error. Nahooin is actually the remnants of another lake situated 200 yards north and is now only a boghole).

The Loch Ness Investigation Bureau had set up camp at the lake with the hope of capturing the monster that had recently been seen both in and out of the lake. Whilst Lionel Leslie, Holly Arnold, Roy Mackal and other members of the expedition were proccupied at the lough's shore, Ted Holiday decided to explore the immediate region to discover the source of the lake's water supply. In Holiday's absence, the otyhers saw a black cat on the opposite shore to them. This was completely unexpected and somewhat ironic – whilst trying to catch a lake monster, they witnessed an unidentified black felid.

What could the wildcat be?

From the aforementioned accounts it is clear that eyewitnesses are seeing some form of felid, but what species could possibly have a tail so pointed that it resembles a nail?

Upon consideration there are several possible identities. An animal which immediately springs to mind is the feral domestic i.e. a once tame domestic tabby which, due to intentional or unintentional neglect, has resorted to living in the wild using its instinct or the descendant of such a cat. It has been observed that feral domestics do not attain a greater size than than their habituated domestic cousins. Also, it would seem that local people would not confuse a tabby with an animal which was not only bigger, but had an extremely sharp (or pointed?) tail which, in certain regions, is supposedly venomous. (This belief may have arisen as a partial attempt to control unruly children).

Another possible explanation may be that local people had attributed to feral cats supernatural physical characteristics, as sometimes happens in folklore. Having said that, there is the possibility that eyewitnesses were attributing sharp tails to the cats because they looked sharp or the tail had partially been uncovered by hair exposing the terminal caudal vertebra.

Another possible identity for the Irish wildcat may be a felid which has originated in a similar manner from another once identified animal – the Kellas cat of Scotland. Again, the standard work on this is Shuker's *Mystery Cats of the World* and his published scientific paper.

The Kellas cat proved to be an animal not without precededent in folklore. In Scottish mythology there was a cat known as the *cat sith*, which was black and possessed sparks on its face. It was also the fairy cat of Highland mythology with a white spot on its breast. The Kellas cat was not only black, but proved to have white guard hairs on its face, which would have seemed like sparks from a distance.

There are indeed reports that suggest a population of Scottish wildcats have in at least one instance been kept in Ireland. At Templemore House in Co Sligo, there have been sightings of large cats in the grounds for many years, which according to eyewitnesses are definitely not feral domestics. The owners allegedly imported true wildcats from Scotland. Apparently the cats are very similar to Scottish cats with bushy, ringed tails and in fact there are some other reports of unidentified cats in Ireland which seem to tally very closely in a morphological way with the Scottish form.

In February, 2002, Sandra Garvey saw an animal while driving at night at Knockfune (Co Tipperary) which shocked her so much she nearly drove off the road. She described it as larger than your average moggy with a very striking tail. It transpired that Mrs Garvey's sighting was not an isolated one, with eyewitnesses coming forth, including park ranger Jimmy Greene who spotted such an animal with its two kittens whilst patrolling the Slieve Bloom Mountains

in Co Offaly. Maybe the necessary circumstances which existed for the Kellas cat to occur i.e. domestic and true wildcats interbreeding have also been present in Ireland for a similar introgressive hybrid to have occurred.

A fascinating programme was shown on the National Geographic Television Channel in 1999 which focused on Madagascar's top predator, the fossa (*Cryptoprocta ferox*). The programme featured Luke Dollar, a biologist from North Carolina's Duke University and one of the foremost experts on this elusive animal. While setting traps for a fossa, he managed to trap another predator – indeed, one that wasn't supposed to exist on the world's fourth largest island – at least not officially.

The animal was a wildcat. What is significant with regard to the Irish mystery is that, not only does this example illustrate that felids are extremely elusive, but also that they can occur in a region (relevantly an island) where, despite being unrecognised by science, they have been known by the indigenous people – sounds familiar.

Also of especial significance with regard to the Madagascan wildcat, known as the *kari* by the Malagasy, is that, upon closer examination of the first captured specimen's mouth, it was evident that this wildcat possessed prominent canines. As will become apparent, this is one of the morphological characteristics that the Irish wildcat possesses according to reports and folklore. There is a report of a wildcat on Inisheer, one of the Aran Islands (Co Galway) with tusks in its mouth.

If ever a specimen of the Irish wildcat becomes available for study, then it might be very close taxonomically to that of the Madagascan animal (DNA results are not conclusive as yet). It has been suggested that the Madagascan felid may be the African wildcat (*Felis sylvestris lybica*) and indeed this was the idea proffered by Dr Scharff in his aforementioned paper.

Conclusions

Maybe the wildcat may prove to be a product of evolution whereby a hybrid resulting from the breeding between Scottish wildcats and feral domestics has produced an animal which may have created recessive genes to become more prominent – thus resulting in very similar appearance to the African wildcat.

Maybe feral domestics have become similar to their African ancestor – with more pronounced physiology including teeth, longer limbs and a more tapering tail. All of these features have been descried by those who claim to have seen the Irish wildcat.

Moreover, the animal responsible for this enigmatic felid may have evolved to fill an ecological niche – in that there are no indigenous predators to keep the ever-increasing population of lagomorphs – particularly rabbits – in check. Rabbits are widespread inparts of Ireland, but are even more evident in coastal dune habitats, very prevalent on the western seaboard.

Even though Stelfox was sceptical as to a separate race or subspecies lying behind the Irish wildcat, this is a situation not without precedent or living examples. The Irish stoat and otter

Pap Murphy is an invaluable resource with regards to the forteana of Co Mayo, and has witnessed identified creatures on occasion. Along with his wife Catherine, Pap is in the process of setting up a folklore centre at their home on the River Mullet.

have evolved over a period of time long enough and in isolation from those on the adjoining island of Britain for them to be recognised scientifically as distinct subspecies.

Or, indeed, from a folklore view maybe the Irish wildcat is nothing more than a coloured, enhanced composite animal, totally unlike its progenitor – the feral domestic. This may have arisen due to superstittious beliefs and a fear of the unknown. For example, there is in Irish folklore an animal called the Faracat – this was said to have been an enormous wildcat with a half-moon colouration on the skin of its back.

Whatever the true identity of the Irish wildcat, it is important to note that, whatever the animal's identity, it will undoubtedly be something different in order for the local population to have distinguished it as something other than the common feral domestic, especially when the cat may have a tail with a hook or nail in it which, according to certain lore, may be venomous. This belief seems to have been prevalent, not only in Co Mayo, but in Co Clare too.

If only the wildcat killed by Pap Murphy's great-uncle had been studied by a zoologist, we would know with certainty its identity.

Brave indeed is the person who would be the first to say he had captured the Irish wildcat – the fella with the nail in its tail.

On the Following few pages we have reprinted
Notes on the Irish Wildcat by Jonathan Downes,
originally published in
Smaller Mystery Carnivores of the Westcountry (CFZ, 1996)

NOTES ON
THE IRISH WILDCAT

*(Thanks to Richard Muirhead for much of the
information included in this appendix)*

The mystery of the Irish Wildcat was discussed briefly in Chapter Two. For the sake of completeness, and also because the subject has only been mentioned once in recent years, [1] we decided to present the available information as an appendix to this present work.

As Karl Shuker points out, the Wildcat is a common figure in Irish mythology. He lists several examples, including an archaic 9th Century poem, translated by Eugene O'Curry and published by Oscar Wilde's father, the notorious Sir William Wilde. This poem tells of the Irish hero, Fin mac Cumhaill, who was held captive by the King of Erinn, who pledged to free him if a male and a female of every wild animal which inhabits Ireland were brought to him as a ransom. [2]

A more recent cultural reference comes in the Shane McGowan song *The Wildcats of Kilkenny*, [3] which retells another ancient legend about a massive battle between the Wildcats of Ireland.

	Locality and Museum Register.		Sex.	Carnassial.	Carnassial to canine.	Carnassial to 1st premolar.	Upper Carnassial.	Remarks.
				m.m.	m.m.	m.m.	m.m.	
Recent in Dublin Museum.	London, ...	43. 1905	♂	7½	32	20½	10½	
	White-park Bay, Co. Antrim,	275. 1902	—	6½	27	18	10	
	loc. (?) (probably Irish), ..	79. 1902	—	6½	23	18	10	
	Dundrum, Co. Dublin, ..	——	♂	7	33½	20	10	
	Cappagh, Co. Waterford, ..	107. 1902	—	6½	30½	20	10½	
	Shot wild at Glenarm, Co. Antrim,	210. 1905	—	6½	29½	18	10	
	Shot wild at Greystones, Co. Wicklow	171. 1896	♂	8	35½	21½	abt. 11	Broken.
Fossil in Dublin Museum.	Edenvale Caves, ..	E. A. 30. ——	—	7	—	19	—	
	" ..	E. C. 230. ——	—	7	29½	19	10	
	" ..	E. C. 93. ——	—	7	27½	18	—	
	" ..	E. C. 230. ——	—	7½	30	19	10½	
	" ..	E. C. 318. ——	—	7	29	19	—	
	" ..	E. C. 87. ——	—	7	—	18	—	
	" ..	E. C. 58. ——	—	6½	—	18	—	
	" ..	E. C. 79. ——	—	7	—	18	—	
Fossil in Dublin Museum.	Newhall Caves, ..	N. H. 34. ——	—	8	34	21	—	
	" ..	N. H. 118. ——	—	8	32½	22½	—	
	" ..	N. H. 156. ——	—	8	—	21½	—	
	" ..	N. H. 102. ——	—	8	32	20	11	Whole skull preserved
	" ..	N. H. 93. ——	—	7½	28	19	—	
	" ..	N. H. 23. ——	—	7½	31	20½	—	
	" ..	N. H. 29. ——	—	7½	30½	20	—	
	" ..	N. H. 2. ——	—	7	29½	20½	—	
	" ..	N. H. 1. ——	—	7	27½	18	—	
	" ..	N. H. 86. ——	—	6½	—	17½	—	
	" ..	N. H. 102. ——	—	6½	24½	16½	—	
	" ..	N. H. 102. ——	—	6½	26	17½	—	
	Barntick Cave, ..	C. B. 7. ——	—	7	27½	19½	—	
	" ..	C. B. 2. ——	—	7	27	18	—	
	" ..	C. B. 6. ——	—	7	27	18	—	
	" ..	C. B. 11. ——	—	6½	28½	18	—	
	" ..	C. B. 2. ——	—	6½	27	19	—	
	" ..	C. B. 6. ——	—	6	26½	17	—	
Recent in Brit. Mus.	England, ..	127. f. ——	—	6½	27	18	10	
	" (tailless var.)	46. 3. 17. 10. ——	—	6½	30½	19	10	
	" ..	41. 7. 14. 46. ——	—	7	26½	18	10½	
	" ..	46. 3. 18. 8. ——	—	8	35½	23	12	
Fossil in Brit. Mus.	Gower Caves, ..	M. 95. ——	—	8	30½	21	—	
	" ..	M. 95. ——	—	6½	20½	18	—	

Tables showing Scharff's finding, first presented in 1905. 1. F. silvestris

LOCALITY AND MUSEUM REGISTER.	Sex.	Lower Carnassial.	Carnassial to canine.	Carnassial to 1st premolar.	Upper Carnassial.
		m.m.	m.m.	m.m.	m.m.
Recent in Dublin Museum. Inverness, Scotland, .. 170. 1899	♂	8	33	21½	10½
Germany, .. 322. 1904	—	8½	36	23	11½
Recent in British Museum. Fort William, Scotland, 99. 2. 9. 1	—	7½	32½	21	10½
Inverness, Scotland, 98. 12. 26. 1	?	8	33½	22	11
,, ,, 4. 1. 25. 3	♀	7½	31	20	10
,, ,, 4. 1. 25. 3	♂	7½	33	22	10½
Caucasus, 79. 11. 15. 4. ——	—	8½	34½	22	11½
Baranza, Hungary, 2. 6. 3. 1	♂	8	35½	22	11½
Manonville, France, 95. 11. 9. 1	♂	8	33	21	11½

Tables showing Scharff's finding, first presented in 1905. 2. F. silvestris

Locality and Museum Register		Sex	Lower carnassial.	Lower carnassial to canine.	Carnassial to 1st premolar.	Upper carnassial.	Remarks.
			m.m.	m.m.	m.m.	m.m.	
Recent in Dublin Museum.	Sardinia, 76. 1901	♂	9	30	20½	12	
	,, 278. 1902	♀	8½	29½	20	11	
	Abyssinia, 549. 1904	—	8½	32	21½	11½	
Recent in British Museum.	Sardinia, 88. 12. 1. 1.	♂	9	34	22½	12½	
	Deelfontein (Cape), 2. 12. 1. 1.	♂	9	36½	24½	12½	
	,, ,, 2. 12. 1. 3	♀	8½	35	22½	11	
	,, ,, 2. 12. 1. 2	♂	9	37	24	12½	
	S. Africa, ,, 857. a	—	9	38½	24	12½	
	Andalusia, ,, 2. 6. 3. 2.	♂	9	37	23	12	
	,, 2. 6. 3. 3.	♀	9½	34½	24	12½	
Fossil in Dublin Museum.	Edenvale Caves, E. A. 42	—	9	32	22½	—	
	,, ,, E. C. 361	—	—	—	—	11	Upper jaw fragment.
	,, ,, E. C. 310	—	8½	—	22	—	
	Newhall Caves, N. H. 88	—	10	36	24½	—	
	,, ,, N. H. 118	—	8½	32½	22	—	
	,, ,, N. H. 88	—	8½	32½	22	—	
	,, ,, N. H. 86	—	8½	—	21½	—	
	,, ,, N. H. 23	—	8½	33	22	—	
	,, ,, N. H. 93	—	—	—	—	12	Upper jaw fragment.
Fossil in British Museum.	Kent's Hole, Torquay, 167. 10	—	8½	33½	22½	—	
	Gibraltar Caves, —	—	9½	—	21	—	
	,, ,, —	—	—	36	21	—	
	Happaway Cave, England, M. 5830	—	—	—	—	12½	Upper jaw fragment.
Oxford Mus.	Kent's Hole, Torquay, —	—	8½	32½	—	—	

Tables showing Scharff's finding, first presented in 1905. 3. F. silvestris

Despite being such a common figure in the folklore of the emerald isle, the actual zoological existence of any indigenous felid within the Hibernian zoofauna is far more problematical.

Karl Shuker noted [4] that William Andrews had noted in the mid-19th Century, that the inhabitants of the more remote glens of Kerry knew of both the Pine Marten and the Wildcat. They had separate names for each. The Pine Marten was known as the 'tree cat' and the Wildcat as the 'hunting cat'. Shuker goes on to list the main eye witness reports of the Irish Wildcat, and presents a useful over-view of the evidence for the continuing existence of an indigenous Irish felid.

Shuker also quotes R.F. Scharff, who, in 1905, presented evidence which suggested that the Irish Wildcat, whether or not it still exists, is more closely allied to the African Wildcat (*F.lybica*), which, at the time Scharff was writing, was known as *Felis ocreata*. His work was concerned with skeletal fragments found in the Edenvale and Newhall caves near Ennis in County Clare.

> *"In examining a number of jaw fragments of cats and single teeth from these caves, I was struck by the great size of the lower carnassials, or molar teeth. Many of the individuals to whom these teeth belonged were evidently domestic cats which had strayed and had died in the caves in recent times, or whose remains had been dragged there by other carnivores. A few, however, seemed to belong to another species, and I determined to make a very careful comparison with all the available material of cats in the Dublin Museum, where, with Mr. Oldfield Thomas' kind permission, I was able to compare them with the large series of cat skulls in his charge. I likewise compared the Irish remains with those of the fossil English Wild Cat remains in the British Museum, Dr. Smith Woodward kindly granting me every possible facility for doing so. And, finally, I examined and measured the well-known jaw of a Wild Cat which is in the charge of Professor Sollas at Oxford, who gladly placed the specimen at my disposal. I have thus had opportunities for handling and critically comparing a large series of the teeth of various species of cats, both fossil and recent.*
>
> *In the following table I give the measurements of the lengths of the lower carnassial teeth of Domestic Cats. In order that there should be no doubt as to the exact position where the tooth was measured, I herewith indicate the line of measurement by a dotted line on a figure representing a carnassial tooth..."* [5]

Scharff continues with a detailed analysis of the findings extrapolated from the above tables. For the cryptozoologist, however, it is his conclusions linking the Irish animals with the African Wildcat, that are most interesting:

> "Only in two cases did this tooth reach a length of 8 mm and both of these were probably old males. They were of powerful dimensions, the skull being quite as large as that of an African Wildcat. One of these was shot as a wild cat in the County Wicklow. It may have been a descendant of a true Wild Cat, which had interbred with the domestic form. In the Gower caves of England, and in Ireland, in the Newhall caves, similar specimens have been met with, which seem to form a link between the Domestic Cat and the larger African Wildcat, in so far as the size of the lower carnassial is concerned. The Domestic Cat may possibly have developed quite independently from the Wildcat in Ireland, and these intermediate stages may be the links connecting the later undoubted cave remains of Domestic Cats with the older ones of the genuine Wildcat"...

From the information presented in the three tables, we have reproduced above, and from the drawings reproduced in the main text of this book, which include comparisons between the jaw bones mentioned above and those taken from mummified cats found in Egyptian tombs, it is hard not to agree with his findings.

Here, one should perhaps mention that in Victorian times, mummified cats from Egypt were imported to Great Britain and Ireland in enormous quantities to be ground up for use as fertiliser. [6] It has been suggested that these are the true origin for the discovery of so many tiny Egyptian artefacts found buried in western European fields, which have, over the years, been used as supportive evidence for some of the most preposterous fortean theories. It is not beyond the bounds of possibility that some of the jaw bones of anomalous examples of *Felis lybica* found in Western Europe may be from this prosaic source.

The enigma of the Irish Wildcat remains, and like so much in that peculiar island, it seems destined to be a mystery for many years to come. Two final feline enigmas remain. The first, fittingly enough, from Scharff:

> "I have met with the remains of an extremely small race of cats in the Newhall and Barntick

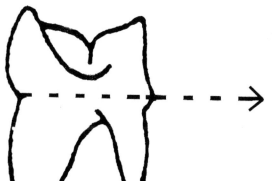

Lower Carnassial Tooth of Cat, showing line of measurement.

caves. The limb bones are about the size of the ordinary Marten (Martes martes), and the lower carnassial, in one case, only measures 5.5 mm in length". [7]

This not only provides supportive evidence for the existence of two marten species in the British Isles, *M.martes* is described as the 'ordinary marten' which implies, quite strongly, that there were two species in the area. It also provides, what is, to my knowledge, the only tantalising fragment of evidence for the past existence of another Irish mystery felid.

A race of tiny Irish cats would be an exciting discovery for any zoologist. It would seem highly likely, however, that they are long since extinct, either by extermination or, more likely, by genetic dilution, a fate which, unfortunately, has probably also overtaken the cat mentioned by Karl Shuker [8] which was:

> *"...of a dirty grey colour, double size of the common house cat and its teeth and claws more than proportionally larger".*

Was this one of Scharff's Irish African Wildcats, or something stranger and even more interesting? Maybe it was the Fairy Cat, the Cait Sidh, described by Shields, [9] and others, given corporeal form, or maybe something wholly new to us all.

REFERENCES

1.SHUKER Dr. K.P.N., *Mystery Cats of the World – from Blue Tigers to Exmoor Beasts* (Hale, London 1989) p. 84 – 89.
2.SCHARFF, R.F., 'On the former occurrence of the African Wildcat (*Felis Ocreata*) in Ireland' (*Proceedings of the Royal Irish Academy* 4.12.1905). p.1.
3.THE POGUES: *Rum Sodomy and the Lash* (STIFF Records 1986).
4.SHUKER Dr. K.P.N., *Mystery Cats of the World – from Blue Tigers to Exmoor Beasts* (Hale, London 1989) p. 85.
5.SCHARFF, R.F., 'On the former occurrence of the African Wildcat (*Felis Ocreata*) in Ireland' (*Proceedings of the Royal Irish Academy* 4.12.1905). pp.1 – 13.
6.TABOR, R. *CATS: The rise of the Cat* (BBC 1991). P.25 – 26.
7.SCHARFF, R.F., 'On the former occurrence of the African Wildcat (*Felis Ocreata*) in Ireland' (*Proceedings of the Royal Irish Academy* 4.12.1905). p.5.
8.SHUKER Dr. K.P.N., *Mystery Cats of the World – from Blue Tigers to Exmoor Beasts* (Hale, London 1989) p. 86.
9.SHIELS, Tony 'Doc', *Monstrum – A Wizard's Tale*. (FT 1987).

11

Paranormal Animals

H ere we come to a rather controversial question. Should paranormal animals be included in the study of cryptozoology?

By this term I cover two types of animal:

- animals that appear to be flesh and blood creatures, but of which it seems unlikely there is a breeding population; an example of this would be, say, the Mothman of West Virginia.
- animals that appear to be of a distinctly spectral nature, e.g., animals that vanish or do not appear solid.

I am only too aware that some cryptozoologists tend to distance themselves from the study of such phenomena. These creatures are beyond the borderline of the current scientific paradigm, they will argue, and if any of them are studied seriously, there is no chance of cryptozoology's ever becoming accepted as mainstream science. Persons taking this viewpoint often feel such creatures are beyond the frontiers of possibility anyway.

A second opinion, to which I myself would adhere, is that such creatures constitute mysterious zooform phenomena and, as such, it is reasonable to investigate their origins, whether these origins lie in fact or fiction. It is true that this attitude is unlikely to get cryptozoology welcomed within the gates of mainstream science with open arms; but we must ask whether such acceptance is truly necessary. First of all, scientists have been wrong about where the boundaries of the possible lie before. Secondly, we should not allow others to tell us what we may or may not study? A desire to fit in with what "the mainstream" thinks is rather like a desire to buy fashionable clothes or designer shoes, not because we like them, but to fit in with the dictates of fashion. Because man is a gregarious animal, it is all too easy for him to yield to pressures to fit in with what the general herd deems acceptable.

Having heard all the above, the reader will, I expect, realise that I intend to look into what

Jonathan Downes calls "zooform phenomena". If you are interested in flesh and blood animals or animals that some would dub of a "realistic" nature, then skip this chapter.

We turn first to Clongowes Wood College, a Jesuit establishment in the east of Ireland. Founded in 1814, it numbers James Joyce amongst its alumni. My grandfather went there and, though he was not in any way paranormal, he was as odd as two left legs. He married my grandmother only because he had shot her brother dead (accidentally, I hasten to add). He was forty and she nineteen. His house was large and plagued with mice. While most people would resort to cat or trap in such circumstances, he blew them out with charges of gunpowder. Finally he blew out the stairs and my grandmother said Enough Was Enough. Clongowes was supposed to be haunted by a hound said to have glowing eyes. It would walk along the corridors by night. Joyce himself mentions it.

If we adjourn to Templeogue in Dublin, we find a place called Pussy's Leap. Despite its name, this place has nothing to do with cats, insofar as I am aware. A large black dog is said to roam the area. As it does so, you can hear its chains rattle.

An heroic figure called Captain Boyd lost his life saving sailors. His Newfoundland dog howled at his grave until it died. It is now said to haunt Glasnevin Cemetary in Dublin.

In Co Donegal the Iskaheen Hound, a sad-looking phantasmal dog, has been seen near Grainne's Gap, Scalp Mountain.

There is a black dog supposed to haunt Slieve Mish (Co Kerry).

In Ireland, black dogs are noted for a propensity to protect fairy sites. One witness said he saw a black dog that looked like a bear. A witness that saw a black dog in Roscommon said its eyes showed almost human intelligence. In 1913 a schoolmaster saw one at Ballygar (Co Galway).

A large black dog is supposed to be on Feltrin Hill at Malahide, to the north of Dublin. So is a phantom grey horse.

North of Dublin lies the town of Howth, where the legendary Finn mac Cool is said to have killed a serpent. Here the ghost of a white rat is said to appear whenever danger threatens the St Lawrence family.

At Castle Biggs (Co Derry) a fire-breathing hound with cloven hooves is supposed to protect hidden treasure.

In 1952, a woman was walking home in the vicinity of Redcross (Co Wicklow). A black dog joined her. When she patted it, her hand went through it.

At the River Quoile, Downpatrick (Co Down), a large, black dog-like creature has been reported.

Stories of black dogs of a phantasmal nature, some friendly, some not, seem quite widespread in England, so it is not surprising to find them in Ireland too. Their nature is certainly paranormal; but, remember, paranormal may simply be taken to mean that which is normal, but which we haven't yet explained.

Equally paranormal is the phantom bull, which is not seen so often. One was seen near Clonlera in 1890. I am told there is one around Lough Derg, but I don't know which of the two lakes of that name.

The classic Irish shapeshifter is the *púca*. Just what it looks like in its natural form is difficult to say. It can appear as a pony, ass, dog, horse or bull. In Fermanagh it is a diminutive humanoid, in Laois a hairy creature and in the south-east of Ireland an eagle. If it is in equine guise and you mount it, it will dash about, but not do you any great harm. Some people think from its name it may be a form of the English *puck* or be related to Old Norse *pukki*, but it is quite possible that, while its name is of foreign origin, it may have been applied to some Irish creature for which there was already a native name. Kennedy tells of one who was originally a man, but had been put into the shape of an ass, in which form he had to do the dishes in a house one night. Hooves, of course, are not suited for such tasks. Kennedy says the headquarters of the *púca* were Carrig-a-Pooka, west of Macroom; Castle Pooka at Doneraile and the island of Melean at the mouth of the Kenmare River.

A phantasmal felid, on the other hand, is the Kilakeel Cat, a giant phantom with red eyes which has been reported from Kilakeel House in the Dublin Mountains.

One of the most frightening creatures of all is the Man-Headed Horse of Louth. This has only been seen once, but once was enough. A couple were driving to Termonfeckin (Co Louth) in 1966 at night, when they saw ahead of them a human-faced horse with bulging eyes. This was near Rath House. The couple's probity was not in doubt. Maybe it is possible that the sudden appearance of the headlights of the car caused an ordinary horse to distort its features in shock, but this seems to me a pretty lame explanation. Funnily enough, a similar creature has been reported from Lincolnshire. This occurred on the ITV programme *This Morning* in the 1990s.

A giant creature resembling a bat is said to have attacked a woman named Kathleen O'Shea near Smerwick on the Dingle peninsula (Kerry) as mentioned in the *Fortean Times* No. 30.

During the 1930s a strange creature, supposedly resembling the chupacabras, was supposed to be in residence in or near the Gougane Barra Forest Park (Co Cork). I have not been able to garner more than the few sparse details mentioned here. My source is the website *Blather*.

Finally, a story taken from Seymour and Neligan, who, alas do not provide locations or dates. The Reverend Bennett, an Anglican minister in Arizona, had friends who had rented a castle in Ireland.

The family, whom the authors simply refer to as the A. Family, settled in, but the servants complained about footsteps outside their doors. Not alone that, someone appeared to be trying to gain entrance to their rooms.

One night, Mrs A. heard footsteps outside her bedroom. Looking out, she beheld a horrible looking face atop the body of an ape. Then it vanished.

Mr A., who had been absent on the night in question, shortly afterwards heard a blood-curdling laugh. Looking up, he saw a figure with a human head of a man of about forty, white and hairless, looking at him over the banisters. The hands and arms looked like those of an ape. The figure was covered with reddish-brown hair.

Sometime afterwards, Mrs A. was arranging flowers, when she felt to hands on her shoulders. Turning around she found herself facing a creature that was, apparently, having a good laugh at her. It was covered with hair like an orang-utan. Mrs A. fainted and a girl coming in saw the creature vanish.

The A. family left the house after this.

12

Hairy Hominids

Does Ireland have any equivalent of the Bigfoot or the Yeti? A look at the size of the country shows us at once that it could not sustain a breeding population of such hominids. This does not mean, however, that such things have never been seen in the country.

There is an Irish word *gruagach* which can mean a magician, giant or ogre. The word *gruagach* actually means 'the hairy one'. The question must be asked if this contains any sort of reminiscense of hairy man-beasts prowling the Irish countryside.

Strange to say, the tradition of the gruagach has not entirely died out and it has been anglicised as grogach, but it is now pictured as a somewhat diminutive being of a paranormal nature. Unlike the leprechaun, however, it does not wear clothes, but is covered by its long hair. This hair – it has sometimes been described as fur – is dirty and tangled and grogochs are said to be of limited intelligence, though not unfriendly. They even had a reputation for helping people with the harvest. They would also help around the house.

They should not, however, be given a reward. This will prevent their returning to the house. They live in what are termed houses, but these are often long leaning stones. They have the power to become invisible. This is a well-known folktale motif. Could any truth lie behind belief in these creatures?

To judge from the fact that the word once meant a giant or ogre, they must once have been considered very large. Patrick Kennedy, the noted folklorist, says they were both gigantic and hairy. The grave of a giant named Gig-na-Gog is supposed to be near Portrush. No evidence has ever been unearthed of a population of such creatures in Ireland. However, there is one possibility which, whatever the reader may think, I cannot overlook.

This possibility is that they have occasionally wandered in from another universe through a portal as yet undiscovered by science. Before the reader feels I am embarking on fantasy here, I would point out that such ideas are no longer as unscientific as once they seemed. Professor Michio Kaku, a physicist whose work has been publicised in recent times, has argued that a plurality of universes may exist, each perhaps budding off from the other. He has even suggested that the human race could at some future date migrate to another congenial universe, though he isn't sure how. He doesn't seem to have considered the possibility that portals already exist, but, if the rest of his ideas are true, such a possibility should not be ruled out.

Is there any evidence of such creatures entering through such portals? Not in Ireland, insofar as I am aware, but such things have been reported elsewhere. For example, in Spottsville (Kentucky) such creatures were seen stepping in and out of a patch of wavy air, as if entering from some parallel world. In Russia there were sightings of wildmen in 1566 and the locals thought they were coming through a nearby portal from another world. Two men actually entered this portal, it was said, and needed help from a hairy man to exit. As is a common motif in folklore, they thought they had been gone for a day, but returned to find twenty years had elapsed since their departure. Today, there have been several sightings of manbeasts in England, notably in the vicinity of Cannock Chase, yet there could not possibly have been a viable population surviving there through the centuries.

The modern grogochs, if any of the above is true, could be a diminutive hairy species, quite distinct from the large hairy beings already alluded to, not unlike the agogwe said to be found in Africa, which flits through portals as the mood takes them. They seem to be well-known on Rathlin Island, in the northerly reaches of Antrim and Donegal. It is just possible that such creatures could exist subterraneously, but they have become so fairy-like in the popular mind that it is hard to distinguish fact from fiction. One tradition ascribes them an Egyptian origin.

In one tale, the gruagach is described as a wizard witha golden crown, but interestingly he comes back and forth from an otherworld, something like the alternative universe mentioned above. Moreover, a gruagach was probably thought of as doughty or strong, as *Gruagach* was once used as a personal name in Louth.

Though actually documented captures of man-sized gruagachs are hardly well-known, a Norse work of the 13th Century entitled *Kongs Skuggsjo* mentions the capture of a wildman in Ireland with a mane running down its back. It was unable to speak.

The Irish gruagach should not be confused with a creature of the same name in Scottish folk-lore, a long-haired beauteous otherworldly maiden. The hairy male gruagach also turns up in Scottish folklore, just to complicate matters.

13

Mermaids

The mermaid is by no means unknown in Irish waters. It is called in Irish *muruach* (which has sometimes been anglicised as 'merrow'). Other Irish words for it include *bruch, muirghein, muirgheilt* and *maighdean mara*. The merman (*fear mara*) is also known in Irish folklore.

An early mermaid in Irish legend was called LiBan, who started life as a mortal human, but, when the waters of Lough Neagh burst out of the well which had contained them, she was

THE MERMAID (FROM VALENTYN)

turned into a mermaid by God, in which state she remained for three centuries. She was then baptised, died and went to heaven.

Mermaids were depicted with fish tails and had sometimes sea-green hair. Each one possesses a *cochailin druith* (a piece of headgear) and, should you snatch it, it cannot return to the sea. There are various stories of humans accomplishing this or stealing a cape, which has the same effect. I should add here that not all mermaids of Irish tradition are tailed: some have feet but these are flatter than humans'. They are said to have webbing between their fingers. There is also a tradition of seal women (called *selkies* in Scotland). They look like seals, but sometimes remove their skins on shore and, if you steal them, the selkie in question cannot return to her watery home. There are several stories of men who have captured mermaids or selkies this way and married them. Invariably the mermaid discovers where her *cochailin* has been hidden and is able to escape. The mermaid in Scotland is supposed to be able to remove her tail to reveal legs beneath and this belief is not entirely unknown in Ireland. An early Irish mermaid is mentioned under the year 1118 in the Annals of the Four Masters where it says she was captured amongst fish at Lis ar Glin between Ossory and Waterford.

With regard to more modern sightings of mermaids in an Irish context, the following tale is found in *Seaweed Memories* by Heinrich Breuer. He asked one Seosamh O Flatharta if he had ever seen a mermaid. He said he had, she was washing herself by the sea shore in the early morning and then she had swum out to sea. She was not half-fish, but a woman all over. Breuer asked if she were not an ordinary girl, but his interlocutor was sure she was not. She was there too early in the morning, he averred. One forms the impression, however, that there was something else about her, for which he couldn't quite find the right phrase, that indicated she was not truly human. He said she was white as snow.

Sea-beings are sometimes reported from Fuagh na mBan in Letterbeg in Connemara. Two men in a currach, according to a report in the *Connacht Tribune* saw a floating object which turned out to look like a man. This angered person growled at them and dived under their currach. They fled and the thing pursued them for 200 yards and then dived into the depths. Locals remembered that a man named Laurence Henry had seen something similar thirty years before.

Lady Gregory was told by a man on the height of Dun Conor that he had heard there was a man fishing on the rocks one time and he had been confronted by a mermaid.

In 1960 two farmers in Ashdee (Co Kerry) claimed they saw a mermaid and were quite sure it was not a seal.

Going much further back in time, the *Freeman's Journal* (April 30th, 1823), reports a young mermaid was cast up on the shore near Dublin, thereby proving the existence of the creature, but as it was going to be exhibited, I suspect it was one of the numerous fakes that are called Jenny Hanivers. These are imitation mermaids and they usually look pretty grotesque.

Many authorities would say that the legend of the mermaid came from sailors who espied dugongs or manatees. What they overlook is that mermaid sightings are often reported from areas where dugong and manatee do not frequent. Moreover, sailors are often well-trained observers and would certainly have to be in an unfit condition to make such a mistake. There are many cases of observations of merfolk, sufficiently close to obviate the possibility of error, which makes one think that there may be some kind of unknown sea-creature, showing remarkably human traits, behind the legend. With regard to the selkies, it has been suggested that the odd Lapp in a kayak, clad in sealskins, may have drifted southwards and, coming ashore in Scotland, given rise to the legend. This viewpoint is argued by J.M. McAulay in his *Seal Folk and Ocean Paddlers* (1998). This does not explain the various mermaid sightings, however. Could it be there is a kind of hominid which adapted to the sea and natural selection led to its legs becoming fused? With regard to breathing underwater, humans can be born with gills, so it is not impossible merfolk could be similarly born – assuming they exist, of course. There are, in Ireland, certain families that claim mermaid ancestry: the O'Flahertys, O'Sullivans and Macnamaras. (The latter, I might add, have no connection with mermaid musical ensembles).

The merman, perhaps because of his less romantic nature, is heard of rather less, but is not unknown. A man named Jack Dogherty in Co Clare was supposed to have seen one. It had green hair, long green teeth, a red nose and pigs' eyes. He donned his *cochailín* and dived into the sea. However, he later met Jack again and took him beneath the water to show him lobster pots in which he had trapped the souls of drowned sailors. The horrified Jack later got the merman drunk and liberated the hapless captives. While this is, of course, a fairy story, it does give a description of what the appearance of mermen was thought to be like.

14

The Dobharchú

[Pronounce *duvarchoo* with *ch* pronounced as in German].

The following chapter on the Dobharchú originally appeared in the Centre for Fortean Zoology Yearbook 2002, *but it has now been fully updated to include new sightings and information and comprises all the information I have on this enigmatic, fascinating Irish mystery animal.*

The most famous mysterious inhabitants of Irish loughs have been reported most frequently for centuries from the western regions of the country, mainly the sparsely populated area of Connemara (Co Galway) where the animals are locally known as horse-eels. There is, however, another very different creature, known as the Dobharchú. In Irish, this word can be used to mean an otter generally, but it has also been applied to a huge breed of otter reputed to have supernatural qualities. It is especially noted in the county of Leitrim between Sligo and Donegal.

Legend, folklore and early accounts

The local population have every reason for being unable to erase this creature from memory and folklore – one of their own was said to have been killed by a dobharchú.

The dobharchú was believed to inhabit a lake known as Glenade Lough located in the southern portion of the county which can be reached by following the R280 northwards from Manor Hamilton to Bundoran. The lough itself is approximately a mile in length and a half mile in

LEFT: The Dobarchu tombstone in its complete form. It measures approximately 4.5ft x 2ft—it is so small that it is relatively inconspicuous - the first time I searched for it I must have eslked walked right over it. Some of the writing can be discerned at the bottom of the tombstone. However, the vast majority of once legible text has unfortunately eroded away over time. Note the lichen growth, which - when I last saw the tombstone - had become progressively worse.

width and is on the left side of the road for some of the road's progression northwards.

Local legend tells of a woman by the name of Grace Connolly (although some versions call her Grace McLoughlin or McGlone as a woman often retained her maiden name in those times) who went to the lough to wash her clothes or bathe. When she failed to return, her husband, Terence, went to search for her. When he found her, she was fatally wounded as presumably mauled. The sight that confronted him must have been terrible, for, lying across his wife's motionless body, was her assailant, a dobharchú. Terence killed the beast; however, its dying cries were sufficient to attract its mate from the lough. This second dobharchú pursued Terence (who was now accompanied by his brother, Gilmartin) who both fled on horseback.

The two men eventually reached a place about twenty miles away called Cashelgarron Stone Fort. They then placed their horses in such a manner as to barricade themselves from the dobharchú whilst they lay hidden waiting for the beast to show. The twenty miles or so of intervening mountainous terrain posed no problem for the dobharchú, as it eventually reached where the two men lay in ambush. In some versions of the story what occurred next must have been savage as the dobharchú killed one of the unfortunate horses and then Terence surprised it, stabbing it mortally.

The event is also commemorated in verse and there are at least two poems dealing with the unhappy death of Grace Connolly by her loathsome assailant.

One of these poems was called *The Old House* and was included in a 1950s collection – *Further Poems* by Katherine A. Fox, who was herself from County Leitrim:-

> *The story told of the dobhar-chú /That out from Glenade Lake/Had come one morning years ago/A woman's life to take.*

The above lines are quite basic, but demonstrate that the event was important (and possibly quite devastating) enough too be recorded in verse in order that its memory should linger.

The second poem is written anonymously and is simply entitled *The Dobharchú of Glenade*, but it goes into greater detail than the first and its entirety consists of sixteen verses and is therefore extremely valuable to the whole legend.

In the aforementioned story we are presented with a rather fanciful local legend, which seems too incredible to believe. However, there is actual evidence for the event's occurrence in the form of Grace Connolly's gravesite. Her grave is located in Conwall Cemetery in the townland of Drummans approximately 2-3 miles from the lake where she met her untimely death.

Upon her gravestone is carved a very unusual animal indeed. It is very like aan otter and a dog, but most intriguingly of all, possesses characteristics of both.

The tombstone is laid in the cemetery horizontally and is approximately 4.5' (135cm) by

ABOVE: Close up of the dobharchú portrayed at the top of Grace Connelly's tombstone. The creature has physical characteristics of both dog and otter. The feature at top right is actually a gloved hand thrusting a spear into the creature's neck. It re-emerges through its underside above the hind paw. The tail of the creature, which apparently had a tuft at the end, has sadly vanished. The thin slice of sandstone to the far left of the dobharchú has disappeared at some point..

BELOW: Glenade Lake. This lake in Co Leitrim was the setting for the terrible death of local woman Grace Connelly by the dreaded
dobharchú or master otter.

Signpost at the side of the R380 between Manorhamilton and Bundoran indicating the location of the dobharchú tombstone. The signpost is no longer present.

2'(60cm). It is made of sandstone and can be located within the cemetery by walking roughly 20' (6.7m) in a northwesterly direction after leaving the small path from the entrance gate. The date on the tombstone is very hard to make out, but it is September 24th, 1722. As can be seen from the photograph, much of the writing has been eroded due to rain and time and most of the tombstone itself is covered with lichens – the large splotches of white and grey.

This animal's strange identikit is as follows. Its hind legs and front legs are equally long and powerful, it has a long tail with a barely discernable tuft at its tip (which has since flaked off) and it also has a deep-set and powerful chest, whereas the creature's small head and paws are very like an otter's, as is its neck, which is doubled over its shoulder and consequently can be missed at first glance. However, its barrel chest and long muzzle are morphologically canine.

One question, which I believe is fundamental from an historic sense is, if the tragic incident did not occur, then why portray the creature in such detail? By comparing dates and styles and other old gravestones in the cemetery, we can determine if Grace did die around 1722. Incidentally, other gravestones which seem to date from the same period as hers have the surname McGlone on them. This is stated to be Grace's husband's surname in some versions of the tale. The cemetery is noted as an ancient monument of interest on an Ordnance Survey map of the region (no. 16 in the Discovery series), A nearly complete signpost still indicates its position from the side of the road.

I took several photographs (which are included here) of both graveyard and tombstone and also took some video footage of the environs. Also intriguing is that the barbed spear grasped by the gloved hand (as can be seen from the enlarged photograph of the animal) enters at the base of its neck above its powerful chest and re-emerges below where its ribcage/stomach would be. This is thought-provoking because if the depicted animal is merely mythical, then why would the stonemason have gone to considerable effort to closely tally his depiction with one of the most significant strands of the alleged event, i.e., the slaying of the dobharchú by the avenging Terence McLoughlin?

Until the First World war (1914-1918) a second dobharchú tombstone existed not too distant from the first, at a townland called Kilroosk. This place is to be found approximately three miles north of Manor Hamilton and can be reached by taking a third class road from the adjoining second class R280 (mentioned above). The second tombstone is also said to have shown a dobharchú, although when Patrick Tohall, who had written on the subject for the Royal Society of Antiquaries in Ireland some time after 1935, made enquiry, the local men referred to it as the Dobharchú Stone and only one man recalled its image, claiming that it was like a horse. It was the gravestone of Grace's husband, Terence. The stone had been placed in a boundary wall, broken and subsequently lost.

The very fact that at one point in time two gravestones existed within the same geographical area demonstrates how significant the event was to the local population. Indeed, for both gravestones to depict the animal which instigated this tragic occurrence is indicative of how unusual such a creature was. Around 1922 the incident was clear in people's minds thereby fortifying the entire occurrence as fact and also the appearance of Grace's assailant.

It is very relevant to summarize the main strands of the legendary and mythical qualities attributed to this enigmatic beast. Firstly, it was believed to have been of unusually large size, sometimes holding court with five or six regular sized otters. Secondly (and possibly significant when trying to identify it with a known group of animals) its mythical qualities included the notion that even the slightest portion of its pelt could save a ship from being wrecked, a horse from drowning or even a man from gunshot or any other serious affliction. Thirdly, it was believed that the animal itself could only be killed by shooting it with a silver bullet (this bizarre notion is uncannily familiar to the werewolf legend). And finally, Patrick Tohall, whilst researching the Dobharchú was informed by an old man in there cords of the Commission for Boundaries, Co Donegal, that an old Irish phrase stated that the Dobharchú is the seventh cub of the common otter. This implies it was a super or master otter. In every usage the word *dobharchú* for the Irish subspecies of otter has been replaced by *mada uisce*, 'water dog'. (There are also several other Irish terms for an otter).

The Dobharchú in Donegal

The Dobharchú is well known in other countries besides Leitrim. To its north lies the relatively large county of Donegal and intriguingly there is also folklore associated with this legendary creature here.

The most gruesome account which happened in the 17th Century, as it is included in old manuscripts, can be found in Joe McGowan's enthralling book *Echoes of a Savage Land* (2002). Within the Atlantic lowland blanket bogland of the Rosses, a Dobharchúallegedly killed and consumed Sheila – a sister of Sean O'Donnell. Sean arrived at the place of the attack – a place named Ros na Ballan – to meet his sister, but tragically found nothing but a heap of bones with his sister's red cloak placed on top. Eventually the Dobharchú travelled inland from the sea one night and lunged at a coat under which Sean was hiding and Sean then killed the animal with some unrecorded weapon.

The account does seem very similar to the incident at Glenade Lough and unfortunately I have been unable to obtain any more details. The Rosses is not only a desolate region of stark remote beauty, but also contains many loughs which would provide more than adequate sanctuary for any elusive animal.

The only other reference to the Dobharchú in Donegal is the one by Captain Lionel Leslie. Whilst in the company of his boatman, Hugh Brennan, Leslie was informed at Lough Derg (not to be confused with the lake of the same name on the Shannon) that there was a rare beast known as the "king of otters".

Dinneen, in his Irish dictionary, while giving *dobharchú* as the Irish for otter, also mentions the giant otter, but seems to think it peculiar to the lore of Donegal.

The once often seen but never captured monster of Sraheen's Lough

When we tend to think of Irish lake monsters we picture images and stories of those equine-headed eel or serpent-bodied creatures aptly named horse-eels. However, some denizens of Irish loughs cannot be categorized in this manner and one of these was sighted in a small body of water on Ireland's largest offshore island – Achill in Co Mayo.

The lough is called Sraheen's Lough (although it also goes by the name of Glendarry Lough). It is roughly circular in shape and approximately 400' (130m) in diameter. When surveyed by Australian students in the late 1960s it was deemed bottomless – possibly the crater of a now-extinct volcano. There are dense rhododendron bushes growing around most of its shoreline and, considering its location on one of the most westerly regions of land in Europe, a more windswept, weather-beaten, isolated wilderness devoid of extensive forestation would be difficult to conceive.

Achill is some 20 miles (32km) long by 14 miles (23km) in width. It possesses mountain peaks over 2000'(620m) high and also the highest sea-cliffs in Europe, where the northern face of Croaghan Mountain drops nearly 2200' (690m) into the Atlantic below. It is not far from Glenade Lake in Co Leitrim, on the mainland.

There was an oral tradition of water monsters in and around Sraheen's Lough. Stories were remembered by the older generation (and used to frighten unruly children!), but in 1968 such stories were to become fortified by an unbelievable series of events which allowed fairytales

Sraheen's Lough on Achill Island, Co Mayo. Also known as Glendarry Lough, it is famous due to the mysterious creature seen in and around it during the 1960s, and even the year 2001

to make the transition from myth into reality.

It all began when two local men, John Cooney and Michael Nulty, were to have an unforgettable experience of a strange creature at the lough on 1st May. They were driving home to Achill Sound on the mainland from the village of Keel when, at about 10 p.m., a bizarre animal ran across the road from the direction of the lake and ran into the thick undergrowth. They were able to see it clearly as it was illuminated by their headlights. They described it as being 8'-10' long (2.4-3m), four-legged, black or dark brown in colour, having a thick tail, a long neck like a swan's and a head like a sheep or greyhound. It was about 2.5'(0.75m) tall and, when it ran, it rocked from side to side. John Cooney also noted it was moving at an angle, weaving and curving and its eyes were glittering. This would suggest the irises of the animal were highly reflective and might be of a mammalian species.

The men's sighting was not an isolated one and only a couple of months later two girls were hitching a lift when on their way to the mainland when they thought that their eyes were deceiving them.

Mary O'Neill who was from Mullingar (Co Meath) and Florence Connaire from Galway were given a lift by a Dundalk businessman (whose identity I have not been able to discover) in June, 1968. Just as they passed the lake one of them noticed a huge animal on the lakeshore, about 100 yards (95m) from their position. The animal was about 20' (6.5m) in length (although the size is doubtless exaggerated), it possessed a head like a greyhound's and a long tail.

The sighting gained notoriety in the Irish press as apparently the businessman stopped and took a photograph of the animal. An enlargement of the photograph was printed in the Dublin *Evening Herald* on June 5th, 1968. Some people consider this was a hoax.

Two years earlier in July, 1966, an Englishman was fishing on the lough. Suddenly the serenity of the lake was disrupted by a commotion on the surface. The fisherman watched in awe as a long neck possessing a swan-like head appeared. The long neck was connected to a shiny black body, which soon emerged. The creature then decided to move towards the petrified angler. The petrified angler then decided to move away from the lake and fled to a shop on Achill Sound, approximately a mile away, owned by Dennis McGowan. Apparently white with fright, he recounted his incredible experience.

Only a week afterMessers Cooney and McNulty's sighting, a fifteen year old boy named Gay Dever, stopped while cycling past the lough on his way home from Mass. He had dismounted from his bike and was pushing it up the slight gradient when he heard splashing sounds. It was early evening and he saw a creature emerging from the lough and climbing a bank. Visibility was still good and he watched the animal "bigger than a horse" (?exaggeration) with a sheep-like head on a long neck, with a long tail and possessing four legs, of which the rear ones were much longer than the front ones and which moved in an unusual fashion, jumping "like a kangaroo" and was about 12'(4m) long.

In addition to these sightings, there were tales of a monster in the lake's being seen before, in the 1930s particularly.

The incidents on Achill Island may seem, at first glance, to be unrelated to the legend of the Dobharchú. However, there is a fascinating link between the two.

An artist's reconstruction produced by Janet and Colin Bord based on the eyewitness accounts of 1968 is strikingly similar to the animal depicted on Grace Connolly's tombstone in Drummane. Both creatures possess the same powerful chest, long tail, muscular legs and doglike (greyhound-like) small head with pointed ears and long paws on both front and hind limbs. The artist's reconstruction is eerily similar, though the one is separated from the other by over 200 years. Is it possible that a specimen of the Dobharchú was alive and well and living on Achill as recently as 1968?

Can its mythical qualities offer clues and a possible solution?

The identity of the animal known as the Dobharchú is not straightforward, as there are many strands entwined in the myth. However, certain of its characteristics may enable its identity to become more apparent when we look at them objectively and from a zoological perspective. First of all, there is the alleged supernatural quality of its pelt. According to legend, an inch of its coat will prevent a ship from being wrecked, a horse from being injured and a man from being wounded, even by gunshot.

I believe this strand of the legend can be linked to a fascinating fact concerning another member of the mustelid family – the sea-otter (*Enhydra lutris*). This endearing mammal has the distinction of possessing the thickest coat of all the mustelids. It has the highest density of hair per square centimetre (126,000 on average) and there is a very important region for this.

Due to the sea-otter's almost exclusive existence in the cold, harsh environment of the Pacific Ocean (it doesn't breed or give birth ashore) it needs to retain body heat as it lacks the insulating layer of blubber possessed by larger marine mammals. In fact, its luxurious pelt was the reason for the sea-otter's near demise in the 18th Century, for trappers killed over 190,000 of them to fill the Russian demand, the value of their coats even exceeded that of the sable.

The primary function of the sea-otter's coat in having such an abundance of hairs (more specifically the guard hairs) is to trap air: the layer of trapped air acts as insulating material. If the Dobharchú had a similarly thick coat, it might give rise to its protective reputation.

Also very notable with regard to the Dobharchú's physical appearance is the belief that that, according to legend, its "white coat" was said to have a black cross on the back. This strange feature was not the only unusual variation with regard to the creature's pelt colour as the tips of its ears and the tuft of its tail were also said to have been black.

I wonder if the legend highlights another feature of the animal's appearance. Certain members of the Mustelidae and notably the stoat (*Mustela erminea*) sometimes develop a white coat in winter as an environmental adaptation. However, such a change in the stoat is not complete as the tip of its tail, the ends of its ears and its paws remain a dark brown colour – sound familiar? This change aids the stoat in camouflage (though it rarely occurs if ever amongst the Irish subspecies).

The belief that the Dobharchú's coat was primarily white would also have been based on sightings of living albino otters, which are themselves very rare. In James Fairley's book on Irish mammals *An Irish Beast Book* the author comments on instances whenever white or partially white otters were reported in Ireland. White otters were witnessed by S.J. Hurley from Killaloe (Co Clare) some time in the late 1800s and interestingly the same individual also saw an otter with a complete white circle around its neck. A number of albino otters were seen in 2009.

Fairley also refers to the Dobharchú. He relates how within Sir Ralph Payne-Galloway's *The Fowler in Ireland* (1882) there were men who devoted themselves to trapping animals for their skins and these men told of a kind of otter known as the "King of Otters" or "Master Otter".

The only major problem in identifying the Dobharchú with an animal similar to a sea-otter is that the latter animal is found only along certain coastlines of the Pacific and not in the Atlantic. However, if a fossil of some sort of sea-otter that once resided in thge Atlantic is ever discovered, we may have some clue as to the origin of the Dobharchú. In fact, there is a fossil otter adapted to the sea called enhydratherium. It lived in the Miocene and early Pliocene Periods and its fossil remains have been found in Europe, particularly parts of France.

It, along with several closely related species in the genus Enhydriodon, could be found around the Atlantic rim from Europe to North America. When alive its appearance was very similar to today's sea-otter, but it possessed a shorter, more robust jaw. Significantly, some species of Enhydriodon exceeded the living-sea otter in length and/or breadth, which is of couerse relevant when we consider a suitable candidate for the Dobharchú. It was exclusively marine. Ultimately one of its evolved descendants would be an excellent candidate for this elusive, enigmatic cryptid, especially when we consider its former geographic range. Ireland would have made a very suitable habitat with its near isolated coastlines.

From the evidence presented above, I believe it is safe to assume that, whatever the Dobharchú is, it must have more than a transient relationship with the intriguing family known as the Mustelids.

Worth mentioning here, I feel, is the Mustelids' tendency towards specific physical attributes., which would assist a great deal in disentangling the mystery of the master otter. According to Sean Ó hEochaidh from Donegal, the master-otter is said to be the seventh cub of a seventh cub and therefore a super-otter, presumably a giant.

The otter's tendency towards gigantism is evident in the fascinating Brazilian giant river otter or saro (*Pterona brasiliensis*). This animal is not only special due to its gregarious behaviour, but also attains a length of 6'(1.8m) or in some instances more. Sadly, this impressive animal's distribution is under threat from poachers and ironically tourism itself as this irreversibly affects the habits of this beautiful creature in its natural environment. The River otter and the sea-otter both show that the genus evolves quite comfortably with greater body size than most mustelids. By being relatively large, the sea otter loses less body heat as it has a larger surface area. It is as long as the European otter (*Lutra lutra*) although much more heavily built.

Other possible identities for the Dobharchú is that it is a giant species or subspecies related to the European otter. This may have been indigenous to Ireland, with strongholds in the western region of the country, primarily Leitrim, Sligo and Mayo but also in Donegal, Roscommon and Galway based on possible sightings reported up to 2003. A genetic bottleneck caused by factors such as inbreeding, geographical barriers (such as mountains or islands) or even recessive genes from its evolutionary history could have resulted in a radically different otter.

Such an otter would possess certain morphological and behavioral characteristics and traits not normally observed in the common Irish otter. Such traits might include gigantism, aggressiveness, greater carnivorous instincts and melanism.

One further point which demonstrates that even modern day otters can exhibit unexpected behaviour can be seen from the following (possibly unique) example which parallels part of the Dobharchú legend.

A pair of giant otters kept at Sao Paolo Zoo in Brazil both took part inkilling a keeper whom they perceived as a potential threat to their young. I have not been able to determine the date of this tragic occurrence, but it should certainly be kept in mind next time an exuberant tourist with a camera seeks to photograph this beautiful animal. There is actually a modern instance of an otter attacking a person in Ireland. In 1936 Ronan Drury was attacked by such a beast in Co Meath. It went for his neck, but was at last driven off by a helpful goose and gander which arrived upon the scene.

The behaviour of the Brazilian otter corresponds to what we are told of the Dobharchú.

The Scottish angle

When we examine the Dobharchú legend we must also examine its existence in the folklore of our north-eastern neighbour, Scotland. A reference to the Dobharchú in Scotland was kindly sourced and forwarded to me by fellow lake monster researcher Nick Sucik, who hails from Minnesota, USA. Nick is very interested in the Irish phenomenon and is well versed with regard to it. I am very grateful to him for the following reference.

Martin, in his interesting *Description of the Western Isles of Scotland* (1703), vol. 8, p.159, tells us that in the Isle of Skye there is a big otter above the ordinary size, with a white spot in its breast, and this they call the king of otters; it is rarely seen and very hard to kill. Seamen ascribe great virtue to its skin, for they say that it is fortunate in battle and that victory is always on its side.

The Isle of Skye and Achill Island would seem to be visited or populated by Dobharchú – examination of vegetation type, topography and flora/fauna present and the surrounding marine ecosystem might prove useful in determining why this animal chose these reasons and why itis scarce.

There is a lake in Scotland called Loch nan Dobhrachan. There was an attempt to catch a monster here in 1870. With a name such as that, it would indicate the monster was a Dobharchú. Forbes tells us there was in Sutherland a certain otter that was either white or dun with a white star and this beast was supposed to be king of the otters.

Literary sources

If anyone were to question the existence of the Dobharchú in Irish legend before its appearance in 1722, then it is significant to mention a man travelling around the west of Ireland by the name of Roderick O'Flaherty whilst collecting stories for his book – *A Description of West or hIar Connaught* (1684). This tells of the Irish Crocodile, which he mentions when writing about Lough Mask:

> *There is one rarity more which we call the Irish Crocodile whereof*
> *one as yet living about ten years ago* [in 1674] *had sad experience.*

The man was passing the shore just by the waterside and spied far off the head of a beast swimming, which he took to be an otter and took no more notice of it, but the beast it seems lifted up its head to discern whereabouts the man then was, then diving swam under the water till he struck ground, whereupon he ran out of the water suddenly and took the man by the elbow whereby the man stooped down and the beast fastened his teeth in his pate and dragged him into the water, where the man took hold of a stone by chance in his way and calling to mind the kniofe he had in his jacket, took it out and gave a thrust of it to the beast which thereupon got away from him into the lake. The water about him was all bloody, whether from the beast's blood or his own or both he knows not. It was the pitch [colour]of an ordinary greyhound, of a black shiny skin without hair as he imagines. Old men acquainted with the lake do tell there is such a beast in it and that a stout fellow with a wolf dog along with him met the like there once, which after long struggling went away, in spite of the man and his dog and was long time after found rotten in a rocky cave of the lake when the waters decreased. The like they say is found in other lakes in Ireland, they call it Dovarchu, i.e., water dog or anchu which is the same.

This animal is unlike the commonplace Irish otter, for although it initially looked like one, it evidently wasn't and it was unfortunate for the person involved that it deemed him a very suitable item for dinner.

Peter Costello, a name with which cryptozoologists are very familiar, was contacted by a woman called Anne Kinsella, from Gorey (Co Wexford). This woman must have communicated with Costello more than once, as he refers to her as "a correspondent of mine". Writing to him on July 5th, 1963, she refers to otters killed by her brother. Her brother had shot otters 7' in length in a lake near Lough Ree, on the Shannon. Costello remarks that otters of this size might account for the legend of the master-otter. The greatest authenticated length in these islands has been 6' (1.83m). Once again we are presented with a tantalising piece of vital evidence for the physical reality of the Dobharchú. However, in the best cryptozoological tradition, no more information or actual remains seem to have been forthcoming.

Is the Dobharchú resident in a pub in Co Mayo?

Whilst travelling to Connemara during April, 1999, to do some research on horse-eels seen in the region's lakes, I stopped with my companions, grandmother (Eilish Donnan) and aunt (Louise Donnan) at a small village named Crossmolina which is in Co Mayo. The village is about five miles from Ballina and is located on the shores of a large lake – Lough Conn. My grandmother told me there was a large stuffed otter in a pub she had visited (in order to use washroom facilities, of course!). This pub is called Hynes Pub and was decorated with old photographs depicting major events of local history dating from the turn of the 20th Century. It also possessed many stuffed animals including the otter positioned above a television. It was very dark in colouration, almost appearing black, and approximately 4.5' (135cm)-

PICTURES ON PREVIOUS PAGE

ABOVE: In this photograph, the stuffed specimen's body looks unusually elongated, and streamlined. The pose of the neck also makes it seem unusually long. This all may be due to bad taxidermy, however, I do feel that somewhere in Ireland, someone may have a giant stuffed otter - the legendary Dobharchú.

BELOW: From this angle the otter has some unusual physical characteristics such as a thick, muscular tail, and strong hind limbs. The specimen's overall length is approximately 4.5ft; about average for European otters.

5'(1.5m) in length. What grabbed my attention even more than its size was its unusual shape. Its neck seemed unusually long and sleek, its hind legs were slightly elongated and, most eye-catching of all, it possessed a long thick bushy tail. This animal differed markedly from the Irish otter.

Some of these very striking physical features may have been partly due to the manner in which the animal was both stuffed and displayed by the taxidermist. However, after a brief examination, I feel that any possibility of intentional tampering by the taxidermist can be ruled out. Unfortunately, I failed to ask the publican or customers anything about the history of the strange looking otter.

As can be seen in the photographs, the interesting morphological characteristics of the specimen are somewhat similar to those depicted on Grace Connolly's tombstone – the Dobharchú. The long bushy tail, strong, slightly elongated hind limbs, muscular chest and lengthy neck are predominent on both animals. Have we here sound zoological evidence for the beast?

Possible sightings post 1968

"Sometimes all it takes is a little patience" – this is a very appropriate axiom in the study of cryptozoology. Whenever I first started to research the Dobharchú legend, I was saddened to discover there had been no sightings of the creature after 1968. Happily I was wrong and, during the course of my researches, I have uncovered several alleged sightings which indicate it is not ready to be labeled "extinct" yet.

The first of these sightings occurred in 1999/2000 near Portumna (County Galway). Patrick Sullivan from Cleggan, Connemara, was driving along the N65 towards Loughrea when he suddenly saw an animal he didn't recognise wandering on the opposite side of the road. He decided to turn at the nearest available opportunity in order to take a closer look at it. He informed Tom Joyce that it was similar to an otter only larger and darker in colour. After a few minutes, his mysterious creature moved away from the road and disappeared into some undergrowth.

The next sighting was at Sraheen's Lough around 2001. I was only aware of it thanks to my colleague and friend from the Mullet – Pap Murphy. Pap told me that the Sraheens Lough

A digital drawing of the Creature we witnessed. © Sean Corcoran 2010

A digital drawing of the Creature we witnessed. © Sean Corcoran 2010

monster had been sighted near the lough at this time and its very existence was debated on Radio na Gaeltachta. I have at present no further details.

"It is always good to leave the best till last" and I believe this is very appropriate in relation to the encounter which happened in Omey Island near the village of Claddaghduff in Connemara in April/May 2003. The island is accessible by car or on foot whenever the tide is out. It boasts two freshwater loughs – the larger is known as Fahy Lough. It was at this lough that Sean Corcoran and his wife Miranda saw something incredible. One night Sean was alerted at about 3 a.m. by a strange yelp or cry coming from the sand dunes at the western side of the lough. He proceeded to where he thought the sounds were coming from and then switched on his head torch. The couple, I should explain, were camping on the island). Suddenly the light illuminated a large animal that Sean described as bigger than his full grown labrador. At this point the creature was only about 2-3 yards away. It then quickly swam from one side of the lake to the other. It then clambered onto a large rock and rose up on its hind legs. When I spoke with Sean in December, 2009, he informed me that the creature was dark coloured and approximately 5'/1.7m in height when on the rock. However, the animal's most intriguing characteristic was its feet, as they were orange or red and described by Sean as flippers rather than feet.

I must point out a couple of things here – first of all, I have always felt there should have been sightings in this lough. This is because it is only about 20 yards from the sea at the sheltered cove in the western part of this unspoilt island. Irrespective of whether Ireland's lake monsters turn out to be oversized individuals of known animals (e.g., giant eels) or whether they are evolved forms of creatures known from the fossil record, the proximity of the sea is part of the puzzle – both are inextricably linked. Secondly, the sea around Omey is still relatively unspoilt with plenty of food available, such as fish and crustaceans. Sean told me that in previous camping stays on Omey he had found scats near the lough, which, when examined, mostly contained the remains of shellfish and crabs. Coincidentally, this is the kind of food

My own artistic reconstruction of the dobharchú/master otter

one would expect a coastal otter to consume – whether it is giant or of normal size.

Daev Walsh in *Blather* (21st August, 1998) says that in Leitrim today the Dobharchú is sometimes regarded as a sort of witch which rules the other water animals.

Zoologically speaking, the discovery of such an animal would demonstrate how a relatively small island such as Ireland could harbour a relatively giant species – whether indigenous or migratory. A specimen would, of course, have to be offered up for formal scientific scrutiny if acquired as exploitation can become a reality of an endangered or new animal as it becomes available to science.

N.B. – The words dhuragoo, dorraghower and doyarchu are merely
attempts to render this name in English.

15

The Dwarf Wolves of Achill

I first learned of the Dwarf Wolves of Achill Island whilst reading the September 1997 issue of *Uri Gellar's Encounters.* (issue no. 12). An article by Dr Karl Shuker entitled *From Liver Birds to Leopard Cats* delves into the mythological animals of Britain and Ireland. On page 22 is a reference to the Achill wolves.

According to Irish tradition, Co Mayo's Achill Island was home to a

type of small wolf-like beast long after true wolves died out elsewhere in the British Isles. They were said to resemble normal wolves in overall appearance, except for their small stature.

Even though I had been aware that my own country (in the more remote regions at least) was said to contain unidentified lake monsters, I was especially thrilled that there was yet another creature that remained unaccepted and undiscovered by the zoological community.

When Dr Shuker's classic book *Extraordinary Animals Revisited* was republished by the Centre for Fortean Zoology in 2007 on page 95 I found it mentioned once again the Dwarf Wolves of Achill. However, on this occasion, he provides the reader with a tantalising new facet of these enigmatic creatures

> *In a letter to me of 21st February, 1998, British zoologist Clinton Keeling provided me with a fascinating snippet of information on this subject – revealing that as comparatively recently as 1904 the alleged Achill Island wolves were stated to be "common" than no less a person as Sir Harry Johnston, discoverer of the okapi.*

One of my regrets is not contacting Clinton Keeling in order to elicit more details. I can't help but wonder about the origins of the exact year he quotes and, of course, how Sir Harry Johnston discovered the mysterious canids in the first place.

Achill – the island of bogs and cliffs

Achill is Ireland's largest offshore island (280 square metres). It is certainly an island of superlatives. It possesses the lowest and highest corrie lakes in the country. Even more spectacxular are the vertiginous cliffs of Croaghaun, which form a 3km precipice on the island's north-eastern end. They drop an incredible 664m/2192 feet sheer into the Atlantic below and as such are more than three times the height of the famous Cliffs of Moher in Co Clare. In fact, they are the highest sea-cliffs in Europe. Achill also has the Menawn Cliffs which extend for approximately 2km and rise to more than 450m/1350 feet for most of their length.

Even though Achill has many awe-inspiring geographical features, its wildlife is sparse to say the least. However, this wasn't always the case, will early naturalists or commentators mentioning the proliferation of animal and bird life in particular. In fact, both the golden and white-tailed sea-eagle existed in astonishing numbers with successful breeding occurring up to the end of the 19th Century. Its varied bird life included chough, snow bunting, ring ouzel, grouse and other raptors such as peregrine falcon, kestrel, merlin and sparrowhawk. Sea birds included razorbills, guillemots, puffins, cormorants, northern divers and gulls. Tragically, the bird life has been persecuted to such an extent that the only places where it can be seen today in ant numbers are the inaccessible cliffs of the island's northern side.

Significantly, certain terrestrial mammals such as foxes, hares and rabbits were also very common at one time. It is important to remember whenever I visited Achill in April, 2009, the only wildlife we saw were some seagulls, sheep, swans and a hare bounding across the road at

Dooagh village. Compare this with the deafening sounds of the 50,000 plus seabirds, golden hares (a unique subspecies), buzzards and 30 or so grey seals we watched one day on Rathlin (Co Antrim)

Other mini-wolves
If there are Dwarf Wolves on Achill, it might be interesting to see if other populations of such diminutive creatures have evolved. Intriguingly, Mother Nature has given us several other forms of dwarf wolf on a couple of occasions. The most famous is the Japanese shamanu (*Canis lupus hodophilax*) which was (and possibly still is) the world's smallest species of wolf, incredibly only 14m at the shoulder and approximately only 45m in length. The reason for its diminutive height is due to its unusually short legs – in fact, this morphological feature was so destructive that some zoologists assigned the shamanu full species status. Even though this miniature wolf was revered by the Ainu people, a group of indigenes who preceded the main Japanese population to the islands, as "the howling god" it was still persecuted by hunting and deforestation. Tragically, the shamanu was declared officially extinct in 1905. However, sightings of small wolves continued after this date with the most striking evidence coming in the form of nineteen photos taken by Hiroshi Yaqi in 1966.

Another miniature wolf was the Falklands Islands wolf (*Dusicyon australis*), which was also vertically challenged, reaching a height of 24m at the shoulder. As with all wolves, the world over, it too was hunted to extermination by early Spanish and Scottish settlers. Sadly, by 1876 it was no more and yet another form of wolf was extinct.

The Hungarian reedwolf was a mysterious and as yet uncategorised canid reported from Hungary and eastern Austria up to 1900. Its identity has never been satisfactorily determined and yet there are specimens in museums around the world. It may even be, not a wolf, but a jackal.

Before leaving the subject of mini-wolves, it is important to note that there were some prehistoric forms. One such example was the small race of wolf indigenous to the Channel Islands off the coast of California. This wolf certainly evolved to take advantage of the abundance of prey, in particular the dwarf mammoths (*Mammuthus exilis*) which were themselves only 6'/1.8m in height.

From the previous accounts it can be seen that the wolf, even though it has suffered considerable assault by man, has adapted and evolved to survive in many habitats. Even more thought-provoking is its occurrence on islands, showing that the alleged Achill wolves would not be unique.

Why are islands zoologically special?
Islands have always exhibited a certain mystique with regard to their ecology and wildlife. In fact, zoologists recognise a process whereby evolution affects the size of island mammals. This rule is known as Foster's Rule and demonstrates that smaller animals tend to increase in size, while larger ones tend to decrease. The reasons for this are relatively straightforward – the smaller mammmals such as mice have less predators to worry about so they can evolve

into larger island varieties, e.g., the St Kildan field mouse (*Mus hirtensis*). Conversely the larger mammal species are restricted by the availability of food and consequently over generations reduce their body size to cope with this fundamental problem.

Significantly, from an evolutionary point of view, why would the European wolf evovlve a smaller version on Achill Island in the first place? As previously mentioned, the island did produce sufficient prey, but the lack of forestation for cover would definitely have been a major problem.

What exactly were Achill's dwarf wolves?

It is worth mentioning here that in Shuker's *Extraordinary Animals Revisited* there is a very intriguing clue to the identity of Achill's dwarf wolves. The possibility that young wolves or even jackals were imported for hunting is very plausible. These small wolves allegedly existed until 1920. The last normal wolf in Ireland was said to have been killed in 1786, though this date has been disputed.

In 2007 I became aware of another possible identity after discussing the subject with my friend and correspondent Pap Murphy.. When I asked him about Achill's dwarf wolves he immediately spoke about the *cordog*. This was a medium-sized dog which apparently was half collie and half terrier.. Pap also informed me that it was fast, ferocious, clever and was used to hunt rabbits at night time. Significant was the once common belief on Achill that wolves and dogs bred (which they can do freely) and the result was the previously mentioned cordog. I am currently trying to obtain a photo of a cordog as the breed is sadly extinct. Therefore, this is possibly the only way to ascertain if there was any morphological relationship with the wolf and, if so, would be the only evidence thus far to help prove the one-time existence of the Achill mini-wolves.

The only other possibility to account for the dwarf wolves would be confusion with foxes. (Intriguingly, at one time on the island foxes were apparently tamed to hunt rabbits). I find this difficult to understand how the ubiquitous fox would be confused with the much-maligned wolf, no matter how large or unusual the fox was.

Now for the ambitious part! Puzzling aspects.

Despite the lack of concrete evidence for this creature's very existence and, indeed, the lack of reports after 1905, I do feel there is a genuine unidentified animal responsible for the dwarf wolf tag. As cryptozoologists are well aware, one of the main obstacles to mainstream scientists' accepting their work, including their research and conclusions, is their over-reliance on anecdotal evidence, i.e., eyewitness accounts. Although there are some good sightings regarding dwarf wolves there are also a few niggling fundamental questions which need to be answered. For example, if there were genuine/bona fide dwarf wolves on Achill, how did they come to be on the island in the first place? Why have no archaeological remains been found to date, considering the amount of digs which occur on the island?

Whenever I started to research the factors which would be required for a population of wolves, dwarf or otherwise, to survive on Achill, I was immediately struck by the lack of habitat in the form of forestation. Crucially, how would a small population not succumb to the problems of disease due to a restricted gene pool as a result of so small a population. How many dwarf wolves existed in Ireland in the first place?

Final thoughts

Frustratingly – perhaps tellingly – Achill's dwarf wolves weren't mentioned by any of the prominent naturalists of the 19th Century, such as Scharff, Stelfox, Barrett or Hamilton. Robert Llloyd Praegar doesn't mention the possibility in his seminal work *The Way That I Went* and, if they were supposedly common until 1900s, this would have been expected. Previously I mentioned the lack of suitable forested areas on Achill. Such would be of course a necessity not only for more effective hunting, but to conceal their dens safely away from other predators and, of course, man. However, there is a forested area on the mainland north-east of Mullarany known as Cartron. Intriguingly, if this area was forested until 1900s, then conceivably a population of dwarf wolves could have traversed Achill Sound at low tide, looking for opportunities on Achill. There is also the possibility that the animals from the mainland were normal-sized Irish wolves and over generations became smaller to adapt to the prey and lack of cover present on the island.

Out of all Ireland's undiscovered animals, the possibility that a form of miniature wolf existed on the country's largest island (which is admittedly small by Scottish standards) some 130 years after the last remaining wolves became extinct is definitely very exciting. How eerie it must have been for Achill's inhabitants to have heard a howl in the dead of night over the incessant sound of the Atlantic crashing at the headlands and base of the precipitous cliffs on Europe's most westerly land.

As I have been unable to discover any newspaper references to dwarf wolves on Achill Island it might be assumed that the belief that they survived to the incredibly recent date of 1910 must have been due to a mistake or another animal altogether.

Dr Kieran Hickey of University College, Galway (National University of Ireland) has conducted extremely thorough research on all aspects of the history of the wolf in Ireland. In fact, it is probably the most extensive study of this much maligned apex predator in the Emerald

Isle. Dr Hickey has a book forthcoming in 2010 which I am eagerly awaiting.

He has informed me that it is very unlikely, almost impossible, that any wolves, whether stunted or regular-sized, survived beyond 1800. The presence of suitable habitat large enough to sustain a genetically viable breeding population free from inbred illnesses coupled with adequate food is lacking. However, he is open-minded concerning the possibility of other as yet undiscovered animals in the remote, underpopulated wilderness areas in Ireland. He believes such animals are individuals that are very distinctive morphologically in one way or another, e.g., in colour, shape and particularly size. For example, he believes the legend of the Dobharchú is based on eyewitness accounts of extremely large individuals within regional populations of the Irish otter. After many years of investigation of this creature, I would be inclined to agree with that proposed identification.

In conclusion, it seems as though regrettably we have reached a dead end in respect of the survival of a dwarf form of wolf on Ireland's largest island – Achill. Unless any archaeological remains are discovered in the future which would conclusively prove its existence, then Achill's vertically challenged wolves will have to remain, as is so often the case in cryptozoology, an enigma – albeit a very fascinating and intriguing one.

16

Big Cats

In recent years there has been what can only be described as an outbreak of sightings of large cats where no such cats are supposed to be. Amongst students of unusual phenomena, they have become known as ABCs (alien big cats). One thinks of the United States, Britain and Australia in this respect. However, there have been some sightings of such cats in Ireland too.

A certain confusion has to be anticipated in evaluating such reports. People have a tendency to label brown cats as pumas and black ones as panthers, but can it really be said the publ;ic are sufficiently *au fait* with such creatures to identify them with certainty? Can your average person distinguish between a puma, a jungle cat, a golden cat, a small lioness or a caracal or can he tell, say, a black panther from a jaguarundi? Moreover, in the United States, jaguars, of which black specimens occur, seem to be making a comeback in Arizona, just to complicate matters. Moreover, some of the big cats reported seem to bear the coloration of domestic cats and one wonders if they are a mutant strain of such animals or even just large housecats misidentified due to perspective?

The puma (*Puma concolor*) is known by a number of other names - the cougar, mountain-lion, mountain cat, catamount, deer tiger, mountain screamer, painter and panther. They are coloured brown. It has sometimes been mooted that there are black specimens, but there is very little evidence for this.

The term panther is more properly used for the leopard (*Panthera pardus*) and generally these days is confined to the black coloured ones. These are leopards with melanism (a black equivalent of albinism) and if you approach one closely you can see the leopard's rosettes against its black skin - not that I would recommend a close approach if you met one in the wild.

Most alien big cats reported have been identified with one or other of these, but one cannot rely too closely on the accuracy of the identification.

There is an early report in the *Anglo-Celt* (September 9th, 1944). This was of a large snow-white animal which killed kittens, birds and small dogs. It is interesting to note that some of the more recent reports from Britain have included large white cats.

One of the earlier reports comes from Ballyvourney (Co Cork) where a beast called the Bally-vourney Cat was seen crossing a road in 1980. It was coloured pale grey and its length was estimated at 2.5'. It was described as shaggy, but not long-haired. Janet and Colin Bord suggest it might have been a lynx. Before one asks what a lynx was doing in Corkonian regions, it might be well to remember that there have been rumours in Britain of hunts introducing and freeing lynxes to use as quarry. Perhaps the same idea occurred to an Irish hunt. However, caution is indicated here. It is not absolutely certain that this animal belonged to the cat family at all. It might have been a dog, for example, seen in peculiar light.

Ulster seems to have had quite a number of reports and it is generally thought such animals have been deliberately released by their owners. One was reported in Tyrone in 1999. Another was reported there on the Favour Royal Road in 2007. In September, 2002, while the USPCA were looking for a puma near Ballybogey, they found prints which they took to be those of a black panther. What was possibly a young puma was reported there in 2003; the possibility of its being a lynx was also suggested. Reports came in of a large cat on the north coast of the province. Police planned a stakeout for a suspected puma in North Antrim, but the animal was frightened off by the unexpected arrival of a car. A day-long search by police with helicopter support and the USPCA proved fruitless. The USPCA said in 2006 they believed two black panthers and three pumas were at large in the north of Ireland.

THE BLACK PANTHER.

To show that not all these animals are of the black panther or puma kind, it might be mentioned that police in Northern Ireland shot a lynx at Fintona in 1996. A possible lion was reported by a number of people on Cave Hill, Belfast, in August, 2008. The Cave Hill is heavily wooded. The Belfast Zoo is there, but there have been no reports of escaped lions.

Going further south, a photograph of what looks like a big cat was taken by Dr Brendan O'Donnell in the Mourne Mountains in July, 2003. It shows a large black/brown animal - the colour in the photograph looks more consistent with that of a black panther than a puma, but questions of shade and light need to be addressed here. Stephen Bradley, a former lion-tamer, said the shape of the tail made him certain it was a black panther.

Co Down, where the Mournes lie, has been the scene of big cat reports for many years. As early as May, 2001, police issued a warning that there was an ABC in the Border area. Teeth marks consistent with such a beast were found in a rabbit in Co Down. A puma or panther origin was suggested. The story was carried in the *Irish Examiner*, 22nd May, 2001.

In 2001 a strange cat with a bushy tail was reported from Redcross (Co Tipperary). In the same year at Blessington (Co Wicklow) a beast which was compared with a cheetah was discerned.

Lest people think that proximity to a city renders them safe from such a creature, a beast that was described as a "puma-like" animal was seen on the Ballybogey Road on 26th September, 2003.

In the Republic, according to the *Irish News* (29th June, 2004), a large black cat was sighted outside Monaghan on June 28th. Gardaí and an army marksman were searching for the animal. There had been reports for several months and locals suspected there were at least two cats in the area.

Returning to Leinster, the *Laois Nationalist* (29th October, 2002) reported an animal spotted by a motorist on the Main Dublin Road. At first the motorist mistook it for a dog. It was wearing a collar. The motorist seems to have considered a cat possibility only some days later and we may have here a perfectly ordinary animal distorted by memory.

An alleged panther, black and the size of a large dog, was seen in the area of Dundrum (Co Tipperary) in 2007. Some time afterwards it was seen in Kilsheelin, Glendale Wood and Coolishad Wood.

A large black cat was discerned in Comeragh Wood (Co Tipperary), but the sighting, which appears in the website *Blather*, is undated. Another Tipperary sighting in Kilcooly Woods occurred around March, 2008.

The *Irish Examiner* (5th February, 2008) carried a report of a black panther in Glanardin Wood (Co Cork).

Way out west in the wilds of Connemara (Co Galway), Caroline King, on 14th September, 2009, saw a large black cat the size of a sheepdog.

While we are on the subject of sheepdogs, in certain cases the finding of sheep carcases has led to people inferring the existence of ABCs. It must be borne in mind that sheepdogs will also sometimes attack sheep, perhaps leading people to blame ABCs. Some farmers, all too well aware of this, have found a solution. Instead of sheepdogs, they use llamas.

In 2007 a large brown and white cat was reported from Donegal. Although it was searched for, it disappeared from human ken. This might point in the direction of a mutant feral domestic, but it might also have been a reported large dog.

In the same county a year later reports started to come in of a large black cat. A photograph of the beast was taken by a resident of Mannorcunningham.

The only conclusion I can draw about all this is that these cats have, in nearly all circumstances, been released pets or are the offspring of such pets, which would indicate a breeding population. Indeed, it is thought the police know the identity of one former owner. In a country like Ireland, where agriculture plays a big role, this is not a happy thought.

Bibliography

Lake Monsters

Costello, P. *In Search of Lake Monsters* (Garnstone, 1974)
Dinsdale, T. *The Leviathans* (Futura, 1966)
Foster, A. *Foster's Irish Oddities* (New Island, 2006)
Gregory, A. *Visions and Beliefs in the West of Ireland* (Smythe, 1992)
Harrison, P. *Sea-Serpents and Lake Monsters of the British Isles* (Hale, 2001).
Holiday, F.W. *The Dragon and the Disk* (Futura, 1974)
Holiday, F.W. *The Great Orm of Loch Ness* (Faber, 1971)
Holiday, F.W. 'Does the Payshta Still Exist?' *Ireland of the Welcomes Magazine* July/August, 1970.
Leslie, L. 'Monsters Reported from Irish waters' *The Field* December, 1965.
Leslie, L. *The Water Horse* (unpublished book)
McEwen, G. *Mystery Animals of Britain and Ireland* (Hale, 1986)
Mackal, R. *The Monsters of Loch Ness* (Futura, 1976)
Radford, B./Nickall, J. *Lake Monster Mysteries* (University Press of Kentucky, 2006)
Shine, A. *Loch Ness?* (Loch Ness Project, 2006)
Shuker, K. *In Search of Prehistoric Survivors* (Blandford, 1995)
Westropp, T.J. *Folklore of Clare* (Clasp, 2000)

The Dobharchú

Fairley, J. *An Irish Beast Book* (Blackstaff, 1975)
McGowan, J. *Echoes of a Savage Land* (Mercier, 2001)
Shuker, K. *The Beasts That Hide from Man* (Paraview, 2003)
Shuker, K. 'In the Spotlight-the Dobharchu' *Strange Magazine* 16, 1995.
Shuker, K. *Mysteries of Planet Earth* (Carlton, 1999)

The Dwarf Wolves of Achill

Fairley, J. *An Irish Beast Book* (Blackstaff, 1975)
Hickey, K. 'Wolf: Forgotten Irish Hunter' *Wild Ireland* May/June, 2003.

Hickey, K. *Where Have All the Wolves Gone?* (forthcoming, 2010)
Shuker, K. *Extraordinary Animals Revisited* (CFZ Press, 2007)
Shuker,, K. 'From Liver Birds to Leopard Cats' *Uri Geller's Encounters* No. 12, 1997

The Irish Wildcat
Coghlan, R. *A Dictionary of Cryptozoology* (Xiphos, 2004)
De Faoite, D. *Paranormal Ireland* (Maverick, 2002)
Scharff, R.F. 'On the Former Occurrence of the African Wildcat' *Irish Naturalists Journal* 1906
Shuker, K. *Mystery Cats of the World* (Hale, 1989).
Stelfox, A.W. 'Notes on the Irish Wildcat' *Irish Naturalists Journal,* July, 1965

General
Ainmneacha Plandai agus Ainmhithe (Oifig an tSoláthair, 1978)
Forbes, A. *Gaelic Names of Beasts* (Oliver & Boyd, 1905)
MacKillop, J. *Dictionary of Celtic Mythology* (Oxford University Press, 1998)
Newton, M. *Encyclopedia of Cryptozoology* (McFarland, 2005)
O hOgain, D. *The Lore of Ireland* (Boydell, 2006)
Wood-Martin, W.G. *Traces of the Elder Faiths in Ireland* (Longmans, Green, 1902)

About the Authors

Gary Cunningham was born in Belfast in 1971. He was educated at Christian Brothers School and St Patrick's High School, Armagh.

He has been a keen cryptozoologist from the age of ten, favouring a hands-on approach which has led him to tread the trackleswx boglands and wilderness of the far west of Ireland, oblivious of mud and rain. He has specialised in investigating the lake monsters of Ireland, leading him to form his own theory of their niche in the ecosystem, and has also looked deeply into traditions regarding the Dob-harchú or Master Otter, a huge lutrine beast said to exist in the western reaches of Connacht and Done-gal. He has collecting large amounts of eyewitness testimony. For this volume he was also granted access to important manuscript material, which has never seen publication, from the Leslie family.

Gary is now a manager at Dunnes Stores. He is married to Deirdre and has two girls, Maebh and Darcy.

Ronan Coghlan was born in Dublin in 1948. He was educated at St Mary's College, Rathmines, and the Blackrock Academy, Dublin.

He holds an MA degree from Trinity College, Dublin, and the Higher Diploma in Education. He has taught in many schools, notably Hawkhurst Court (Sussex) and Rockport (Co Down).

He has a wide number of interests including folklore and legendary history. His publications include *The Encyclopaedia of Arthurian Legends, Handbook of Fairies, Dictionary of Irish Myth and Legend* and *A Dictionary of Cryptozoology*. He has also contributed to *Tuck's Encyclopedia of Science Fiction and Fantasy* and the online *Almanach de Bruxelles*.

Ronan lives in Bangor, Northern Ireland, with his wife, Mourna, his three children, Lara, Kieran and Ivona, and a dog and a cat who exist in mutual hostility.

Index

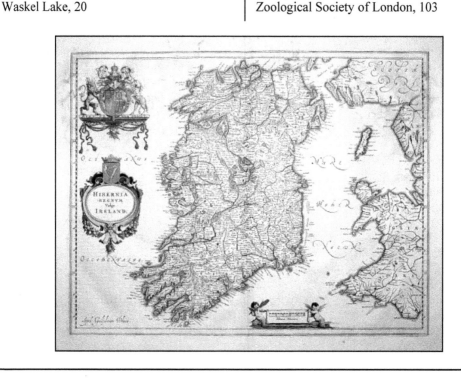

THE CENTRE FOR FORTEAN ZOOLOGY

So, what is the Centre for Fortean Zoology?

We are a non profit-making organisation founded in 1992 with the aim of being a clearing house for information, and coordinating research into mystery animals around the world. We also study out of place animals, rare and aberrant animal behaviour, and Zooform Phenomena; little-understood "things" that appear to be animals, but which are in fact nothing of the sort, and not even alive (at least in the way we understand the term).

Why should I join the Centre for Fortean Zoology?

Not only are we the biggest organisation of our type in the world, but - or so we like to think - we are the best. We are certainly the only truly global Cryptozoological research organisation, and we carry out our investigations using a strictly scientific set of guidelines. We are expanding all the time and looking to recruit new members to help us in our research into mysterious animals and strange creatures across the globe. Why should you join us? Because, if you are genuinely interested in trying to solve the last great mysteries of Mother Nature, there is nobody better than us with whom to do it.

What do I get if I join the Centre for Fortean Zoology?

For £12 a year, you get a four-issue subscription to our journal *Animals & Men*. Each issue contains 60 pages packed with news, articles, letters, research papers, field reports, and even a gossip column! The magazine is A5 in format with a full colour cover. You also have access to one of the world's largest collections of resource material dealing with cryptozoology and allied disciplines, and people from the CFZ membership regularly take part in fieldwork and expeditions around the world.

How is the Centre for Fortean Zoology organised?

The CFZ is managed by a three-man board of trustees, with a non-profit making trust registered with HM Government Stamp Office. The board of trustees is supported by a Permanent Directorate of full and part-time staff, and advised by a Consultancy Board of specialists - many of whom are world-renowned experts in their particular field. We have regional representatives across the UK, the USA, and many other parts of the world, and are affiliated with other organisations whose aims and protocols mirror our own.

I am new to the subject, and although I am interested I have little practical knowledge. I don't want to feel out of my depth. What should I do?

Don't worry. We were *all* beginners once. You'll find that the people at the CFZ are friendly and approachable. We have a thriving forum on the website which is the hub of an ever-growing electronic community. You will soon find your feet. Many members of the CFZ Permanent Directorate started off as ordinary members, and now work full-time chasing monsters around the world.

I have an idea for a project which isn't on your website. What do I do?

Write to us, e-mail us, or telephone us. The list of future projects on the website is not exhaustive. If you have a good idea for an investigation, please tell us. We may well be able to help.

How do I go on an expedition?

We are always looking for volunteers to join us. If you see a project that interests you, do not hesitate to get in touch with us. Under certain circumstances we can help provide funding for your trip. If you look on the future projects section of the website, you can see some of the projects that we have pencilled in for the next few years.

In 2003 and 2004 we sent three-man expeditions to Sumatra looking for Orang-Pendek - a semi-legendary bipedal ape. The same three went to Mongolia in 2005. All three members started off merely subscribers to the CFZ magazine.

Next time it could be you!

Project Kerinci, Sumatra - 2003
In search of the bipedal ape Orang Pendek

How is the Centre for Fortean Zoology funded?

We have no magic sources of income. All our funds come from donations, membership fees, works that we do for TV, radio or magazines, and sales of our publications and merchandise. We are always looking for corporate sponsorship, and other sources of revenue. If you have any ideas for fund-raising please let us know. However, unlike other cryptozoological organisations in the past, we do not live in an intellectual ivory tower. We are not afraid to get our hands dirty, and furthermore we are not one of those organisations where the membership have to raise money so that a privileged few can go on expensive foreign trips. Our research teams, both in the UK and abroad, consist of a mixture of experienced and inexperienced personnel. We are truly a community, and work on the premise that the benefits of CFZ membership are open to all.

What do you do with the data you gather from your investigations and expeditions?

Reports of our investigations are published on our website as soon as they are available. Preliminary reports are posted within days of the project finishing.

Each year we publish a 200 page yearbook containing research papers and expedition reports too long to be printed in the journal. We freely circulate our information to anybody who asks for it.

No. Each year since 2000 we have held our annual convention - the *Weird Weekend* - in Exeter. It is three days of lectures, workshops, and excursions. But most importantly it is a chance for members of the CFZ to meet each other, and to talk with the members of the permanent directorate in a relaxed and informal setting and preferably with a pint of beer in one hand. Since 2006 - the *Weird Weekend* has been bigger and better and held on the third weekend in August in the idyllic rural location of Woolsery in North Devon.

Since relocating to North Devon in 2005 we have become ever more closely involved with other community organisations, and we hope that this trend will continue. We also work closely with Police Forces across the UK as consultants for animal mutilation cases, and we intend to forge closer links with the coastguard and other community services. We want to work closely with those who regularly travel into the Bristol Channel, so that if the recent trend of exotic animal visitors to our coastal waters continues, we can be out there as soon as possible.

We are building a Visitor's Centre in rural North Devon. This will not be open to the general public, but will provide a museum, a library and an educational resource for our members (currently over 400) across the globe. We are also planning a youth organisation which will involve children and young people in our activities.

Apart from having been the only Fortean Zoological organisation in the world to have consistently published material on all aspects of the subject for over a decade, we have achieved the following concrete results:

- Disproved the myth relating to the headless so-called sea-serpent carcass of Durgan beach in Cornwall 1975
- Disproved the story of the 1988 puma skull of Lustleigh Cleave
- Carried out the only in-depth research ever into the mythos of the Cornish Owlman
- Made the first records of a tropical species of lamprey
- Made the first records of a luminous cave gnat larva in Thailand
- Discovered a possible new species of British mammal - the beech marten
- In 1994-6 carried out the first archival fortean zoological survey of Hong Kong
- In the year 2000, CFZ theories were confirmed when an new species of lizard was added to the British list
- Identified the monster of Martin Mere in Lancashire as a giant wels catfish
- Expanded the known range of Armitage's skink in the Gambia by 80%
- Obtained photographic evidence of the remains of Europe's largest known pike
- Carried out the first ever in-depth study of the *ninki-nanka*
- Carried out the first attempt to breed Puerto Rican cave snails in captivity
- Were the first European explorers to visit the `lost valley` in Sumatra
- Published the first ever evidence for a new tribe of pygmies in Guyana
- Published the first evidence for a new species of caiman in Guyana
- Filmed unknown creatures on a monster-haunted lake in Ireland for the first time
- Had a sighting of orang pendek in Sumatra in 2009
- Published some of the best evidence ever for the almasty in southern Russia

EXPEDITIONS & INVESTIGATIONS TO DATE INCLUDE:

- 1998 Puerto Rico, Florida, Mexico *(Chupacabras)*
- 1999 Nevada *(Bigfoot)*
- 2000 Thailand *(Giant snakes called nagas)*
- 2002 Martin Mere *(Giant catfish)*
- 2002 Cleveland *(Wallaby mutilation)*
- 2003 Bolam Lake *(BHM Reports)*
- 2003 Sumatra *(Orang Pendek)*
- 2003 Texas *(Bigfoot; giant snapping turtles)*
- 2004 Sumatra *(Orang Pendek; cigau, a sa-bre-toothed cat)*
- 2004 Illinois *(Black panthers; cicada swarm)*
- 2004 Texas *(Mystery blue dog)*
- Loch Morar *(Monster)*
- 2004 Puerto Rico *(Chupacabras; carnivorous cave snails)*
- 2005 Belize *(Affiliate expedition for hairy dwarfs)*
- 2005 Loch Ness *(Monster)*
- 2005 Mongolia *(Allghoi Khorkhoi aka Mongolian death worm)*
- 2006 Gambia *(Gambian sea monster , Ninki Nanka and Armitage's skink*
- 2006 Llangorse Lake *(Giant pike, giant eels)*
- 2006 Windermere *(Giant eels)*
- 2007 Coniston Water *(Giant eels)*
- 2007 Guyana *(Giant anaconda, didi, water tiger)*
- 2008 Russia *(Almasty)*
- 2009 Sumatra *(Orang pendek)*
- 2009 Republic of Ireland *(Lake Monster)*
- 2010 Texas *(Blue dogs)*

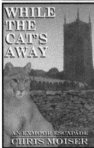

Other books available from
CFZ PRESS

CFZ PRESS

THE SMALLER MYSTERY CARNIVORES OF THE WESTCOUNTRY
Jonathan Downes - ISBN 978-1-905723-05-8

£7.99

Although much has been written in recent years about the mystery big cats which have been reported stalking Westcountry moorlands, little has been written on the subject of the smaller British mystery carnivores. This unique book redresses the balance and examines the current status in the Westcountry of three species thought to be extinct: the Wildcat, the Pine Marten and the Polecat, finding that the truth is far more exciting than the currently held scientific dogma. This book also uncovers evidence suggesting that even more exotic species of small mammal may lurk hitherto unsuspected in the countryside of Devon, Cornwall, Somerset and Dorset.

THE BLACKDOWN MYSTERY
Jonathan Downes - ISBN 978-1-905723-00-3

£7.99

Intrepid members of the CFZ are up to the challenge, and manage to entangle themselves thoroughly in the bizarre trappings of this case. This is the soft underbelly of ufology, rife with unsavoury characters, plenty of drugs and booze." That sums it up quite well, we think. A new edition of the classic 1999 book by legendary fortean author Jonathan Downes. In this remarkable book, Jon weaves a complex tale of conspiracy, anti-conspiracy, quasi-conspiracy and downright lies surrounding an air-crash and alleged UFO incident in Somerset during 1996. However the story is much stranger than that. This excellent and amusing book lifts the lid off much of contemporary forteana and explains far more than it initially promises.

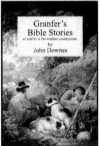

GRANFER'S BIBLE STORIES
John Downes - ISBN 0-9512872-8-1

£7.99

Bible stories in the Devonshire vernacular, each story being told by an old Devon Grandfather - 'Granfer'. These stories are now collected together in a remarkable book presenting selected parts of the Bible as one more-or-less continuous tale in short 'bite sized' stories intended for dipping into or even for bed-time reading. `Granfer` treats the biblical characters as if they were simple country folk living in the next village. Many of the stories are treated with a degree of bucolic humour and kindly irreverence, which not only gives the reader an opportunity to re-evaluate familiar tales in a new light, but do so in both an entertaining and a spiritually uplifting manner.

FRAGRANT HARBOURS DISTANT RIVERS
John Downes - ISBN 0-9512872-5-7

£12.50

Many excellent books have been written about Africa during the second half of the 19th Century, but this one is unique in that it presents the stories of a dozen different people, whose interlinked lives and achievements have as many nuances as any contemporary soap opera. It explains how the events in China and Hong Kong which surrounded the Opium Wars, intimately effected the events in Africa which take up the majority of this book. The author served in the Colonial Service in Nigeria and Hong Kong, during which he found himself following in the footsteps of one of the main characters in this book; Frederick Lugard – the architect of modern Nigeria.

CFZ PRESS, MYRTLE COTTAGE,
WOOLFARDISWORTHY BIDEFORD,
NORTH DEVON, EX39 5QR
w w w . c f z . o r g . u k

Other books available from
CFZ PRESS

CFZ PRESS

ANIMALS & MEN - Issues 1 - 5 - In the Beginning
Edited by Jonathan Downes - ISBN 0-9512872-6-5

£12.50

At the beginning of the 21st Century monsters still roam the remote, and some-times not so remote, corners of our planet. It is our job to search for them. The Centre for Fortean Zoology [CFZ] is the only professional, scientific and full-time organisation in the world dedicated to cryptozoology - the study of unknown ani-mals. Since 1992 the CFZ has carried out an unparalleled programme of research and investigation all over the world. We have carried out expeditions to Sumatra (2003 and 2004), Mongolia (2005), Puerto Rico (1998 and 2004), Mexico (1998), Thailand (2000), Florida (1998), Nevada (1999 and 2003), Texas (2003 and 2004), and Illinois (2004). An introductory essay by Jonathan Downes, notes putting each issue into a historical perspective, and a history of the CFZ.

ANIMALS & MEN - Issues 6 - 10 - The Number of the Beast
Edited by Jonathan Downes - ISBN 978-1-905723-06-5

£12.50

At the beginning of the 21st Century monsters still roam the remote, and sometimes not so remote, corners of our planet. It is our job to search for them. The Centre for Fortean Zoology [CFZ] is the only professional, scientific and full-time organisation in the world dedicated to cryptozoology - the study of unknown animals. Since 1992 the CFZ has carried out an unparalleled programme of research and investigation all over the world. We have carried out expeditions to Sumatra (2003 and 2004), Mongolia (2005), Puerto Rico (1998 and 2004), Mexico (1998), Thailand (2000), Florida (1998), Nevada (1999 and 2003), Texas (2003 and 2004), and Illinois (2004). Preface by Mark North and an introductory essay by Jonathan Downes, notes put-ting each issue into a historical perspective, and a history of the CFZ.

BIG BIRD! Modern Sightings of Flying Monsters

Ken Gerhard - ISBN 978-1-905723-08-9

£7.99

From all over the dusty U.S./Mexican border come hair-raising stories of modern day encounters with winged monsters of immense size and terrifying appearance. Further field sightings of similar creatures are recorded from all around the globe. What lies behind these weird tales? Ken Gerhard is a native Texan, he lives in the homeland of the monster some call 'Big Bird'. Ken's scholarly work is the first of its kind. On the track of the monster, Ken uncovers cases of animal mutilations, at-tacks on humans and mounting evidence of a stunning zoological discovery ignored by mainstream science. Keep watching the skies!

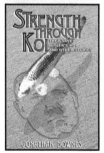

STRENGTH THROUGH KOI
They saved Hitler's Koi and other stories

£7.99

Jonathan Downes - ISBN 978-1-905723-04-1

Strength through Koi is a book of short stories - some of them true, some of them less so - by noted cryptozoologist and raconteur Jonathan Downes. The stories are all about koi carp, and their interaction with bigfoot, UFOs, and Nazis. Even the late George Harrison makes an appearance. Very funny in parts, this book is highly recommended for anyone with even a passing interest in aquaculture, but should be taken definitely *cum grano salis*.

CFZ PRESS, MYRTLE COTTAGE,
WOOLSERY, BIDEFORD,
NORTH DEVON, EX39 5QR

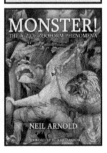

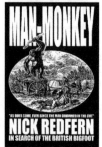

Other books available from
CFZ PRESS

CFZ PRESS

Other books available from
CFZ PRESS

CFZ PRESS

BIG CATS IN BRITAIN YEARBOOK 2008
Edited by Mark Fraser - ISBN 978-1-905723-23-2

£12.50

People from all walks of life encounter mysterious felids on a daily basis, in every nook and cranny of the UK. Most are jet-black, some are white, some are brown; big cats of every description and colour are seen by some unsuspecting person while on his or her daily business. 'Big Cats in Britain' are the largest and most active research group in the British Isles and Ireland. This book contains a run-down of every known big cat sighting in the UK during 2007, together with essays by various luminaries of the British big cat research community.

CFZ EXPEDITION REPORT 2007 - GUYANA
ISBN 978-1-905723-25-6

£12.50

Since 1992, the CFZ has carried out an unparalleled programme of research and investigation all over the world. In November 2007, a five-person team - Richard Freeman, Chris Clarke, Paul Rose, Lisa Dowley and Jon Hare went to Guyana, South America. They went in search of giant anacondas, the bigfoot-like didi, and the terrifying water tiger.

Here, for the first time, is their story...With an introduction by Jonathan Downes and forward by Dr. Karl Shuker.

CENTRE FOR FORTEAN ZOOLOGY 2003 YEARBOOK
Edited by Jonathan Downes and Richard Freeman
ISBN 978 -1-905723-19-5

£12.50

The Centre For Fortean Zoology Yearbook is a collection of papers and essays too long and detailed for publication in the CFZ Journal *Animals & Men*. With contributions from both well-known researchers, and relative newcomers to the field, the Yearbook provides a forum where new theories can be expounded, and work on little-known cryptids discussed.

CENTRE FOR FORTEAN ZOOLOGY 1997 YEARBOOK
Edited by Jonathan Downes and Graham Inglis
ISBN 978 -1-905723-27-0

£12.50

The Centre For Fortean Zoology Yearbook is a collection of papers and essays too long and detailed for publication in the CFZ Journal *Animals & Men*. With contributions from both well-known researchers, and relative newcomers to the field, the Yearbook provides a forum where new theories can be expounded, and work on little-known cryptids discussed.

**CFZ PRESS, MYRTLE COTTAGE,
WOOLFARDISWORTHY BIDEFORD,
NORTH DEVON, EX39 5QR
w w w . c f z . o r g . u k**

Other books available from
CFZ PRESS

CFZ PRESS

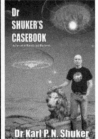

Other books available from
CFZ PRESS

CFZ PRESS

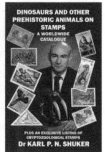

Dinosaurs and Other Prehistoric Animals on
Stamps: A Worldwide Catalogue
Dr Karl P.N.Shuker - ISBN 978-1-905723-34-8

£9.99

Compiled by zoologist Dr Karl P.N. Shuker, a lifelong, enthusiastic
collector of wildlife stamps and with an especial interest in those that
portray fossil species, it provides an exhaustive, definitive listing of
stamps and miniature sheets depicting dinosaurs and other prehistoric animals issued by countries throughout the world. It also includes sections dealing with cryptozoological stamps, dinosaur
stamp superlatives, and unofficial prehistoric animal stamps.

CFZ EXPEDITION REPORT 2008 - RUSSIA
ISBN 978-1-905723-35-5

Since 1992, the CFZ has carried out an unparalleled programme of research and
investigation all over the world. In July 2008, a five-person team - Richard Freeman,
Chris Clarke, Dave Archer, Adam Davies and Keith Townley went to Kabardino-
Balkaria in southern Russia in search of the almasty, maybe mankind's closest relative. Here, for the first time, is their story...With an introduction by Jonathan Downes
and forward by Dr. Karl Shuker.

CENTRE FOR FORTEAN ZOOLOGY 2009 YEARBOOK
Edited by Jonathan Downes and Richard Freeman
ISBN 978 -1-905723-37

£12.50

The Centre For Fortean Zoology Yearbook is a collection of papers and
essays too long and detailed for publication in the CFZ Journal *Animals
& Men*. With contributions from both well-known researchers, and relative newcomers to the field, the Yearbook provides a forum where new
theories can be expounded, and work on little-known cryptids discussed.

THE MYSTERY ANIMALS OF THE BRITISH ISLES:
KENT
Neil Arnold
ISBN 978-1-905723-36-2

£12.50

Mystery animals? Great Britain? Surely not. But is is true.

This is a major new series from CFZ Press. It will cover Great Britain and the
Republic of Ireland, on a county by county basis, describing the mystery animals of the entire island group.

**CFZ PRESS, MYRTLE COTTAGE,
WOOLFARDISWORTHY BIDEFORD,
NORTH DEVON, EX39 5QR
w w w . c f z . o r g . u k**

Other books available
from
CFZ PRESS

CFZ PRESS

GIANT SNAKES
By Michael Newton
ISBN: 978-1-905723-39-3

£9.99

In this exciting book, Michael Newton takes an overview of the most terrifying uberpredators in the world - giant snakes. Outsized examples of known species as well as putative new species are looked at in detail.

THE MYSTERY ANIMALS OF THE BRITISH ISLES:
THE WESTERN ISLES
Glen Vaudrey
ISBN 978-1-905723-42-3

£12.50

Mystery animals? Great Britain? Surely not. But is is true.

This is a major new series from CFZ Press. It will cover Great Britain and the Republic of Ireland, on a county by county basis, describing the mystery animals of the entire island group.

Strangely Strange but Oddly Normal
Andy Roberts
ISBN 978-1-905723-44-7

£14.99

An anthology of writings from one of Britain's most respected Fortean authors, covering everything from UFOs, to the Rolling Stones, and from psychedelic drugs to ancient fertility symbols, the Incredible String Band, and government cover-ups.

China: The Yellow Peril?
Richard Muirhead
ISBN 978-1-905723-41-6

£7.99

Richard Muirhead takes an in depth look at the history of Western relationships with China. If some Victorian antiquarians are to be believed contact between the Chinese Empire and other Middle Eastern and Western Empires goes back to times long before the birth of Christ, such as the ancient Egyptians and the Roman Empire.

**CFZ PRESS, MYRTLE COTTAGE,
WOOLFARDISWORTHY BIDEFORD,
NORTH DEVON, EX39 5QR
w w w . c f z . o r g . u k**

Other books available from
CFZ PRESS

CFZ PRESS

Tony 'Doc' Shiels

MONSTRUM! A Wizard's Tale
By Tony `Doc` Shiels
ISBN-13: 978-1905723553

£9.99

A timely reprint of the classic account of monster raising by Tony 'Doc' Shiels, once the Wizard of the Western World, and still the Shamrock Shaman. Owlman, Nessie, Morgawr and much more. This new editikon includes a new `postface` by Doc himself and hitherto unseen illustrations. A fantastic book which has rightly become somewhat of a legend.

Edited by Jon Downes

Animals & Men collected Editions Vol 4 *New Horizons*
Edited by Jonathan Downes
ISBN: 978-1-905723-56-0

£12.50

At the beginning of the 21st Century monsters still roam the remote, and sometimes not so remote, corners of our planet. It is our job to search for them. The Centre for Fortean Zoology [CFZ] is the only professional, scientific and full-time organisation in the world dedicated to cryptozoology - the study of unknown animals. Preface by Richard Freeman and an introductory essay by Jonathan Downes, notes putting each issue into a historical perspective, and a history of the CFZ.

RICHARD FREEMAN
ILLUSTRATED BY ANTHONY WALLACE

THE GREAT YOKAI ENCYCLOPAEDIA
By Richard Freeman
ISBN: 978-1-905723-54-6

£14.99

A breakthrough volume for the CFZ. Richard Freeman produces the first ever English language encyclopaedia of Japanese monsters. Lavishly illustrated with classic engravings and specially commissioned artwork by Antony Wallace

KEN GERHARD NICK REDFERN

The Monsters of Texas
By Ken Gerhard and Nick Redfern
ISBN **978-1-905723-57-7**

£12.50

Texas, the Lone Star State - largest, and in many ways the strangest state of the USA. It is the home of monsters like the so-called chupacabras, bigfoot, mystery cats, big birds and more, and two of Texas' best known investigators have teamed up to write about them.

CFZ PRESS, MYRTLE COTTAGE,
WOOLFARDISWORTHY BIDEFORD,
NORTH DEVON, EX39 5QR
w w w . c f z . o r g . u k

Lightning Source UK Ltd.
Milton Keynes UK
UKHW012005281118

333148UK00004B/218/P